SKIRT-A-DAY
SEWING

CREATE
28 SKIRTS
FOR A
UNIQUE LOOK
EVERY DAY

Nicole Smith

PHOTOGRAPHY BY
Peter LaMastro

FRIDAY

SATURDAY

 Storey Publishing

The mission of Storey Publishing is to serve our customers by publishing practical information that encourages personal independence in harmony with the environment.

EDITED BY
Beth Baumgartel and Nancy D. Wood
ART DIRECTION AND BOOK DESIGN BY
Carolyn Eckert
TEXT PRODUCTION BY
Jennifer Jepson Smith

COVER AND INTERIOR PHOTOGRAPHY BY
© Peter LaMastro, except for pages 14,
17, 18, 20, 63, and green background
throughout by Mars Vilaubi

WARDROBE STYLING BY
Anka Itskovich/See Management

HAIR AND MAKEUP STYLING BY
Spring Super/Ennis Inc.

ILLUSTRATIONS BY Ruth Krueger

INDEXED BY Nancy D. Wood

Storey books are available for special premium and promotional uses and for customized editions. For further information, please call 1-800-793-9396.

Storey Publishing
210 MASS MoCA Way
North Adams, MA 01247
www.storey.com

Printed in China by R.R. Donnelley
10 9 8 7 6 5 4 3 2 1

LIBRARY OF CONGRESS CATALOGING-IN-PUBLICATION DATA
Smith, Nicole, 1979–
  Skirt-a-day sewing / by Nicole Smith.
    pages cm
  Includes index.
  ISBN 978-1-60342-974-0 (pbk. : alk. paper)
  ISBN 978-1-61212-245-8 (ebook)
  1. Skirts. I. Title.
TT540.S58 2013
646.4'37—dc23

                                   2012043003

Storey Publishing is committed to making environmentally responsible manufacturing decisions. This book was printed on paper made from sustainably harvested fiber.

SKIRT-A-DAY
SEWING

SUNDAY

MONDAY

TUESDAY

WEDNESDAY

THURSDAY

CONTENTS

Introduction   10

Chapter 1   Gear Up   12

Sewing Tool Kit: Stock up on the essentials   14

Pressing Tool Kit: Key items for precision ironing   18

Patternmaking Tool Kit: What you need to have on hand   20

Chapter 2   Construction Zone   22

Fabric Know-How: Navigating the material world   24

Pressing Matters: Getting the best results from your iron   26

What's the Deal with Interfacing? The inside story   27

Hand Stitches: For fine touches a machine can't handle   28

Seams Your Way: Join your pieces with style   30

Adding the Details: Shape your skirts with ease   35

Closing Time: Sew great-looking closures   38

The Bottom Line: Master hems for a pro finish   45

Chapter 3   Draft Your Own Custom Patterns   52

Body Measurements: Great patterns start with accurate measurements   54

Draft a Customized Skirt Sloper: The building block for your own designs   56

Basic Sloper Design Variations: Get started with designing   64

Finishing Up: What to add before you start sewing   71

Using Your Sloper: How to make the skirts in this book   73

Index   234

WRAP

STRAIGHT

FLARED

HIGH-WAISTED

A MONTH OF SKIRTS!

	SUNDAY	MONDAY	TUESDAY
Chapter 4 **Wrap Skirts** Draft the Basic Pattern 76	**1** Spot On Wrap Patch Pockets and Contoured Waistband 80	**2** Pocket Change Center-Front Opening and Military Bellows Pockets 85	**3** Spring-Loaded Wrap Ruched Waistband, In-Seam Pockets, and Optional Appliqué 91
Chapter 5 **Straight Skirts** Draft the Basic Pattern 118	**8** Twiggy Button-Front Closure 123	**9** Great Scot Knife Pleats 129	**10** High Definition Waist Stay and Hemline Flare with Vertical Panels and Godets 134
Chapter 6 **Flared Skirts** Draft the Basic Pattern 162	**15** Girlie Show Full Hemline and Gathered Waist 166	**16** Lone Star Sheer Overlay and Lining 171	**17** Line-by-Line Flared Vertical Panels 176
Chapter 7 **High-Waisted Skirts** Draft the Basic Pattern 198	**22** Jazz Age Trumpet Silhouette 201	**23** Coney Island Sailor-Style Front Opening 205	**24** French Toast Gored Pockets 211

WEDNESDAY	THURSDAY	FRIDAY	SATURDAY
4 **Double-Time Wrap** Reversible Skirt and Scalloped Hem 98	**5** **Strong Suit** Asymmetrical Hemline 102	**6** **Quick Draw** Tucks and Lining 107	**7** **Frill Seeker Wrap** Flounces 111
11 **Block Party** Contrast Panels 138	**12** **New Wave** Asymmetrical Darts and Elasticized Back Waistband 142	**13** **Super Fly** Fly Front with Belt Loops 147	**14** **Velvet Crush** Pegged Silhouette and Yoke 156
18 **Heavy Metal** Inverted Box Pleats 181	**19** **Piece Gathering** Ruched Panels and Faced Waistline 185	**20** **New Twist** Twisted Bubble Hemline 189	**21** **Violet Femme** Faced Pleats 193
25 **Happy Hour** Button Tab Closure 216	**26** **Nip and Tuck** Release Tucks 220	**27** **Hit the Sack** Paper-Bag Waistline and Sash 224	**28** **Tough Luxe** Asymmetrical Opening and Welt Pocket 228

INTRO-
DUCTION

There are few things that are more creatively satisfying than wearing something I created with my own two hands. Whether it's simply a tote bag that took an hour, or a garment that I slaved over for weeks, being able to respond to compliments with a simple, "Thanks! I made it myself," creates a sense of pride that few accomplishments can match.

Once you learn how to sew, you never look at garments quite the same way again. You start noticing the building blocks it takes to put those incredible frocks together, such as darts, curves, corners, and zippers. While working in the fashion departments for magazines such as *Seventeen* and *Teen People*, I found myself in the fashion closet, turning garments inside out, analyzing every bit, often confusing my coworkers. I was taking Polaroids of interesting zippers, odd seam treatments, cool pockets, fun color combos, and more. I am fascinated by clothes, from their inside out.

When the opportunity came for me to combine my love of sewing and fashion editorial experience as a sewing editor, I jumped at the chance. I adore sewing, and I am greatly passionate about passing on that creative outlet. This book is an extension of that need to pass on what I know to anyone who is thinking about creating their own designs. You can absolutely make the fashions that live in your head a reality — all you need are a few basics under your belt, and I'm here to help get you started.

The very first piece of clothing I made that I actually wore out of the house was a skirt made from a non-stretch cotton fabric. It was a simple A-line wrap skirt made with a Simplicity pattern on my mother's sewing machine from the '70s. The very first pattern I ever drafted was also a skirt. A skirt is the perfect project to help you get your footing in pattern-drafting and sewing, as they're easy to fit and typically simple to sew (of course you can make your design as complicated as you like).

Here you'll find everything you need to start creating custom-fit skirts designed by you, including an explanation of all of the tools you'll need and detailed instructions on how to put the pieces together. The beauty of creating skirts is that once you get one or two under your sewing belt, you'll be able to crank them out like a pro in no time. Start by drafting the basic building block (or sloper) pattern with the instructions found in chapter 3, and from there you'll discover so many variations on the following pages, that you'll be able to wear a new design every day of the month. Another great thing about skirts is that they can usually be drafted and sewn in a day or so, making them instantly gratifying. You can truly make a skirt a day.

Think of these projects as a springboard for your own designs, and experiment as you go. As you become more confident, combine the techniques and push them as far as you can take them. If you want to add a detail that's not in a particular project, do it! Become your own designer. And when someone asks you where you found that fantastic skirt, you can smile and humbly say you designed it yourself.

Nicole

chapter 1

GEAR
UP

Are you ready to start creating your own skirt designs? Whether you're new to sewing and pattern-making or returning after time away, this chapter will explain the supplies you'll need to design and create your own clothes.

One of the best things about design and sewing is that you don't need a lot of expensive tools and equipment to get started, but there are a few things you should have on hand to help get the job done. Before you make your first fabric cut, read this chapter to determine if there are any sewing and patternmaking tools you might already have. Then make a list of the things you want to purchase before you start, and a list of the items that would be nice to have, but can wait awhile.

Take the time to stock up your sewing and patternmaking kits because successful sewing starts with the right tools.

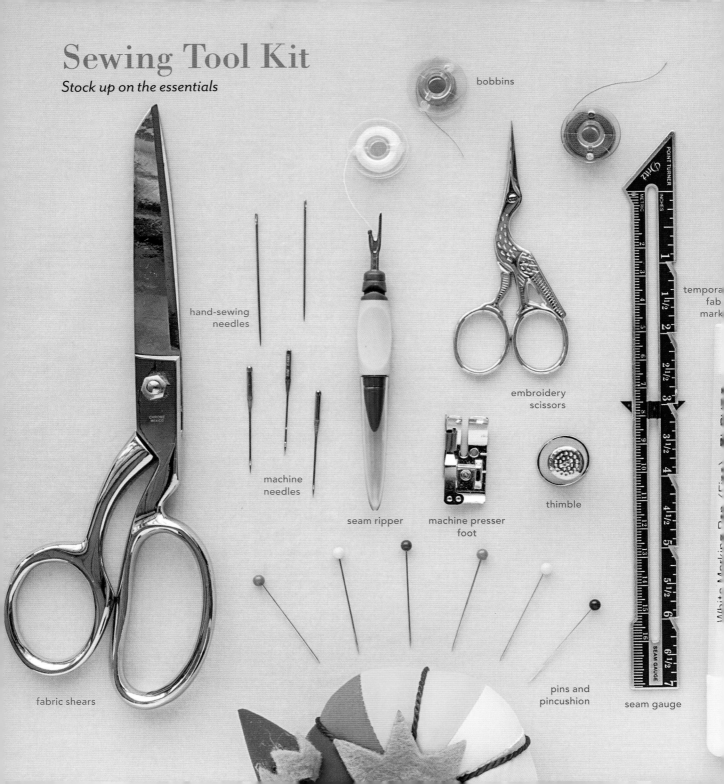

Sewing Tool Kit
Stock up on the essentials

bobbins

hand-sewing
needles

machine
needles

seam ripper

embroidery
scissors

machine presser
foot

thimble

temporar
fab
mark

fabric shears

pins and
pincushion

seam gauge

The following is a list of the tools I consider essential and like to keep on hand in my sewing room. Dull scissors and pins can damage fabric, but it's not important to purchase expensive new scissors or fancy sewing tools if you already have some that work well. It's easy to be overwhelmed by the selection of gadgets at your local sewing store, so keep your budget in mind while shopping and stick to your list.

Bobbins. Make sure you are using the right type and size bobbin for your sewing machine (check your manual or call the manufacturer). Using the wrong bobbin can cause serious damage to your machine. Keep several on hand.

Embroidery scissors or other small scissors. These help you make small cuts and snip into tight places where traditional shears can't reach. They are typically about 4" long and have two sharp points.

Fabric shears. Invest in a good pair of fabric scissors and use them only to cut fabric or you'll dull the blades. Shears are between 7" and 8" long and have bent handles with different size holes for the thumb and the fingers.

Hand-sewing needles. Keep an assortment on hand to accommodate various fabrics and threads.

Iron and ironing board. Good pressing is essential for fine sewing, so investing in a good iron and a sturdy ironing board will save you time in the long run. Look for an iron with easily adjustable heat and steam settings. For more on pressing tools, see page 19.

Machine needles. There are many different type and size sewing machine needles for all the different fabric fibers and weights. See Machine Needle Sizes and Machine Needle Types on the next page.

Pins and pincushion. Straight pins should glide easily through fabric without much effort. If your pins are dull and you have to apply pressure to pierce the fabric, replace them to prevent any fabric damage. Keep a pincushion nearby for easy access to your pins.

Presser feet. Presser feet hold your fabric steady and guide it under the needle and through your machine. Consult your manual for how to install presser feet and what types fit your machine. Most machines come with all of the presser feet you need to create the designs you'll find in this book. Check to make sure you have a general-purpose foot, zipper foot, piping foot, and buttonhole foot. Some extra feet that you might find helpful include an invisible-zipper foot that makes sewing invisible zippers a breeze, and a straight-stitch foot that will help you sew sheer fabrics without rippling.

Seam gauge. This is a small ruler for measuring seam allowances and hems.

Seam ripper. We all make mistakes. Fortunately, a seam ripper can help undo most stitching mishaps. Seam rippers should cut thread easily. If you find yourself pushing hard to break stitches, it's time to replace the ripper.

Temporary fabric marker. There is a variety of fabric-marking tools, including chalks, water-soluble markers, and air-soluble pens. Always test your marker on a fabric scrap to make sure the markings are entirely removable before using it on your garment pieces.

Machine Needle Sizes

Sewing machine needles are often sold in packages with a variety of sizes, since you need different size needles for different fabrics. The needle size is indicated on the package and typically includes two numbers. The higher the numbers, the larger the needle. The first number is the needle shaft's diameter in millimeters. The second number is its U.S. standard size. Choose the needle to best suit your fabric, so that it glides easily through the fabric layers and makes smooth, even stitches.

Fine silks and sheer fabrics	60/8
Lightweight fabrics	70/10
Medium-weight fabrics	80/12
Medium- to heavyweight fabrics	90/14
Heavyweight fabrics	100/16
Upholstery fabrics	110/18

Machine Needle Types

Other than the needle size, you also need to select the correct type of needle.

Ballpoint needles are used with knit fabrics because they have a rounded tip to glide past the fabric's fibers, as opposed to piercing through them.

Denim needles are heavy duty with a sharp tip to allow for easy stitching through thick fabrics such as denim, vinyl, upholstery, and canvas.

Embroidery needles are made especially for machine embroidery and embellishment techniques.

Leather needles have a wedge-shaped point to help them pierce leather and suede.

Metallic needles may seem best for sewing metallic fabrics, but they are really made for use with metallic threads.

Sharp-point (Microtex) needles have very sharp points to stitch flawlessly through silks, microfibers, fine cottons, and other woven fabrics.

Topstitching needles have a larger eye to accommodate thicker topstitching threads. They're also strong enough to pierce multiple layers of fabric.

Universal needles are standard and suitable for sewing most projects, especially those made of medium-weight fabrics.

THREAD

Take care when choosing thread for your design. Not only should you consider color, but you should also keep fiber and thread type in mind. There are many types of thread, all with various purposes. All-purpose thread is suitable for a lot of different sewing projects. For more specific sewing techniques and with specialty fabrics, the threads listed here will work beautifully.

All-purpose thread. Generally a cotton/polyester blend with good stretch; suitable for most garment and home décor projects.

Cotton thread. Cotton thread is made of 100% cotton fibers and is best suited for piecing a quilt or sewing lightweight natural fibers. Mercerized cotton thread has a polyester core and almost no stretch, making it good for natural woven fibers.

Extra-fine thread. Suitable for use with sheer and very lightweight fabrics. Mercerized cotton thread has a polyester core and almost no stretch, making it good for natural woven fibers.

Monofilament thread. This thread is almost invisible and looks a lot like fishing line. It is made of polyester and/or nylon fibers in various shades, including white and gray.

Rayon thread. Rayon thread has a bright sheen and is available in a large variety of colors. Use it for embellishment stitching. It is not suitable for construction because it breaks easily.

Quilting thread. Hand or machine quilting threads are not recommended for garment construction, but for quilting a finished quilt.

Silk thread. Silk thread, available in different weights, is strong and smooth with a nice sheen. It works well for construction, and is the perfect complement to finer-quality fabric.

Topstitching and buttonhole thread. These threads are thicker than all-purpose threads or heavy-duty thread and are available in various fibers. When using these threads in the machine needle, use all-purpose thread in the bobbin in a matching color.

Upholstery thread. Upholstery thread is heavy-duty. It is not recommended for garment construction.

silk   rayon   polyester   upholstery

topstitching   mercerized   all-purpose   fine

monofilament   quilting   cotton

Pressing Tool Kit

Key items for precision ironing

point presser/clapper

sheer organza
pressing cloth

tailor's ham

In addition to your iron and ironing board, there are a few other tools that will help with effective pressing. If you only invest in one extra pressing tool, make it a press cloth, but the other items listed here will help you shape flat fabric into a three-dimensional garment.

Clapper. A clapper is made from wood and is used to flatten fabric after it has been pressed. It's great for setting hems and pleats in place. To use, quickly apply the clapper over the pressed area and apply pressure. The clapper will absorb heat and moisture from the fabric, setting the press perfectly in place. Apply firm pressure with the clapper for a crisp finish.

Point presser. This tool is great for pressing small areas such as collar points and waistband corners. It's not so sharp that it will poke through fabrics and it's iron-safe so you can press over it.

Press cloth. A press cloth is used between your fabric and your iron. It protects your fabric from the iron's direct heat, preventing fabric damage such as unwanted shine and impressions from seam allowances.

Tailor's ham. A tailor's ham is a firmly stuffed pillow that is shaped like a ham. Traditionally, it is stuffed with sawdust, making it firm. It is used to press curved seams, darts, and other curved garment details because it mimics the body's natural curves.

TIP I use a scrap of white, silk organza fabric for my press cloth, which is inexpensive and easy to store. I like that it is transparent, so I can see where I'm pressing, and it's strong enough to withstand the iron's heat.

MASTER TOOL LIST

SEWING TOOL KIT
- Bobbins
- Embroidery scissors
- Fabric shears
- Hand-sewing needles
- Iron and ironing board
- Machine needles
- Pins and pincushion
- Presser feet
- Seam gauge
- Seam ripper
- Temporary fabric marker
- Thread

PRESSING TOOL KIT
- Clapper
- Point presser
- Press cloth
- Tailor's ham

PATTERNMAKING TOOL KIT
- Awl
- Clear tape
- Curved rulers
- Drafting or patternmaking paper
- Eraser
- Gridded pattern paper
- Marking tools
- Measuring tape
- Notcher
- Paper scissors
- Pushpins
- Spiked tracing wheel
- Transparent ruler

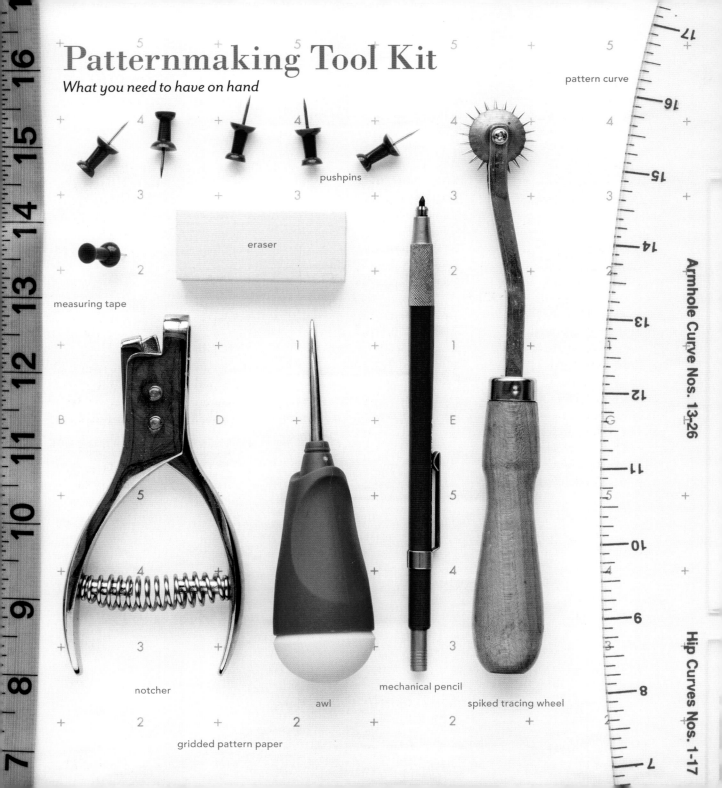

Patternmaking Tool Kit

What you need to have on hand

pattern curve

pushpins

eraser

measuring tape

Armhole Curve Nos. 13–26

Hip Curves Nos. 1–17

notcher

awl

mechanical pencil

spiked tracing wheel

gridded pattern paper

When you start designing your own patterns, there are a few tools that are worth the investment. Some of them might be a little pricey; however, they last for years. If you have trouble locating them at your local chain fabric stores, check online for greater selection.

Awl. Use an awl to mark points on your pattern, such as the ends of darts, buttonholes, and pocket placements.

Clear tape. Keep a roll of clear tape around to mend any accidental cuts in your pattern and for certain patternmaking techniques.

Curves. There are many curved rulers available. I recommend using a vary form or hip curve for drafting skirts. Some manufacturers make larger French curves that will work as well.

Drafting or patternmaking paper. Paper — available in large sheets or rolls — is necessary for most patternmaking, for tracing pattern pieces, and for certain techniques such as slashing and spreading.

Eraser. Keep a large eraser on hand to delete any marking mistakes.

Gridded pattern paper. This pattern paper is printed with a 1" grid to help with measuring and squaring design lines.

Marking tools. Mechanical pencils, because they are precise and erasable, work well, but marking tools are a personal preference. It does help to gather a few pencils and pens in various colors to mark things that need attention.

Measuring tape. A measuring tape is flexible to allow for taking body and dimensional measurements and for measuring curved pattern pieces.

Notcher. This tool isn't necessary, but it's handy to have in the sewing room. It quickly cuts a ¼" × ¹⁄₁₆" notch into the paper, which works well for marking pleats, darts, seam allowances, and more.

Paper scissors. Keep a pair of scissors separate from your fabric scissors for cutting paper, tape, and more. Go ahead and label them so you don't mix them up.

Pushpins. When altering patterns flat on the table, pushpins help you pivot the paper on the table. Just make sure you put down either a cutting mat or a piece of cardboard to protect your work surface.

Spiked tracing wheel. A spiked tracing wheel resembles the tracing wheels you traditionally see in the fabric store. This version, however, has pointy spikes along the wheel to help you trace around designs and transfer them to paper quickly and easily.

Transparent ruler. A transparent ruler with ⅛" grids printed on it works well for most measuring jobs and is flexible for measuring curves.

chapter 2

CON-
STRUC-
TION
ZONE

Once you've assembled your tools, it's time to start designing and sewing. In this chapter, you'll learn the basic sewing techniques you'll need to know to assemble your own skirts, starting with selecting the right fabrics. You'll also learn how to apply interfacing, press correctly, and finally, how to stitch like a pro.

Fabric Know-How

Navigating the material world

The wonderful world of fabrics is gorgeous; it boasts of silks, brocades, sateens, tweeds, metallics, and much more. However, before you venture out into the material world, make sure you know what you're looking for. The selection can be overwhelming, but with a little bit of fabric knowledge under your belt, you're sure to make the choices that will get you just the look you want.

IDENTIFYING WOVEN AND KNIT FABRICS

This book focuses on creating skirt patterns specifically for woven fabrics, so for the techniques demonstrated, knit fabrics will not work. Knits are stretchy and generally require different methods of pattern drafting and sewing. Woven fabrics are traditionally not very stretchy (unless they are made with stretch fibers, such as Lycra), and use techniques, such as darts and gathers, to shape a garment to contour around body curves.

If you're unsure in the fabric store whether the fabric you are considering is knit or woven, take a closer look. A knit is made from looping one continuous yarn around itself. Usually you can spot the loops upon closer inspection. A woven fabric is made from multiple threads that are woven together in a variety of patterns.

woven

knit

PREPPING YOUR FABRIC AND INTERFACING

Before you cut out your fabric, wash and dry it the same way you want to wash and dry the finished garment. If you make your garment from unlaundered fabric, you run the risk of it shrinking and distorting in the wash.

Press your fabric to remove all creases and wrinkles before cutting it.

It's also beneficial to prewash interfacing because it can shrink at a different rate from the fabric and then distort the garment pieces. Even fusible interfacing should be prewashed. To do this, soak your interfacing in a bowl of warm water until the water cools down to room temperature. Then lay out the interfacing on a flat surface to air-dry. For more on interfacing, see page 27.

UNDERSTANDING GRAIN

Grain is the direction of the threads or yarns in woven fabrics, and it dramatically influences the drape

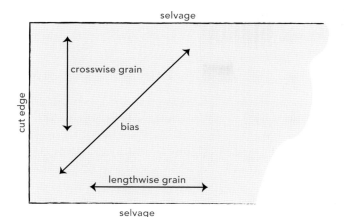

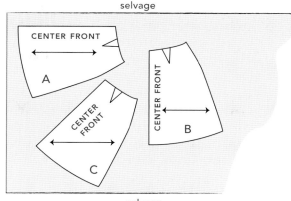

and fit of your garments. It's important to understand how it works.

Woven fabrics have a lengthwise grain, crosswise grain, and bias direction.

It's very important to decide which direction you want to cut your pattern pieces and mark them accordingly. Typically the long arrow on a pattern refers to its "grainline." The pattern is positioned on the fabric with the arrow parallel to the selvages, so it is the arrow placement on the pattern that determines the grainline of the cut fabric.

A: The **lengthwise (or straight) grain** runs parallel to the fabric's selvage (finished edge). There is little or no stretch on the lengthwise grain.

If the arrow runs up and down the pattern piece, parallel to either the center front or the center back of the garment, the garment is cut on the straight grain. Most pattern pieces are cut this way.

B: The **crosswise grain** runs across the fabric from selvage to selvage. There is a small amount of give, or stretch, along the crosswise grain.

When the arrow runs across the pattern, the pattern is cut on the crossgrain and will stretch slightly.

C: The **fabric bias** is a 45-degree angle from the selvage. Fabric has the most stretch along its bias.

If a pattern's grainline arrow is angled so that the pattern will be positioned on the bias, the garment will cling closer to the body and have a very fluid drape.

Mark the desired grainline on all your pattern pieces before cutting them from fabric. Of course, it's up to you which direction you want to cut out your pattern pieces. In the Block Party Skirt on page 138, the striped fabric is cut in different directions to create an original motif.

CUTTING FABRIC

Make sure you cut out your garment pieces using the correct grain. If the grainline is off, the drape of your garment can shift and hang incorrectly on your body.

To pin your pattern pieces on the desired grain, make sure the grainline arrow on the pattern is equidistant from the fabric selvage throughout the length of the pattern. Measure and pin the grainline to the fabric first and then pin the rest of the pattern, smoothing the pattern as you pin.

MARKING THE FABRIC

Once you have your pattern pieces cut out, it's time to transfer the important construction marks from your pattern to the fabric. This includes any registration marks or sewing lines, such as darts, or pocket and zipper placements. Make sure you test your marking tools on a scrap of fabric first to make sure you can remove the marks later (you don't want to accidentally stain your garment before you even wear it). Feel free to use any marking tool that feels comfortable to you, shows up on your fabric, and won't be visible from the right side of the completed garment.

Pressing Matters
Getting the best results from your iron

Great sewing starts with precise pressing. When making a garment, you'll spend about the same amount of time at the ironing board as you will at the sewing machine. Pressing can make the difference between a garment that looks handmade and one with a professional finish.

Pressing your garment during construction isn't quite like ironing a garment to wear. Pressing is an up-and-down motion that helps set your stitch with pressure, heat, and sometimes steam. Ironing, which is the moving of the iron back and forth across the fabric, might distort or stretch new seams. So, don't move the iron across your stitches and fabric; instead, set your stitch with a press.

Before touching the iron to your fabric, consider the fiber content and test press a small swatch to make sure the heat-setting doesn't cause any heat damage, such as shrinking, staining, and even melting.

Fibers and Iron Temperature Settings

Acetate, Acrylic High heat can melt these fibers, so a low heat setting with no steam is best. Use light pressure when pressing to avoid permanent creases.

Cotton, Hemp, Linen These fibers can withstand high heat and steam, so crank up the heat setting and use plenty of steam.

Nylon Nylon is synthetic and can melt. Always use a low heat setting and no steam.

Polyester Polyester can usually withstand medium heat settings and some steam. Avoid firm, hot pressing, which can crease.

Rayon Press rayon fabrics with the iron set on a synthetic setting or medium heat with low steam.

Silk Choose a low heat setting and no steam. Water spots can stain silk.

Wool Select a low heat setting, but you can use high steam.

What's the Deal with Interfacing?

The inside story

Garments are often made of many layers that play supporting inside roles. Interfacing is the layer that adds strength at stress points, such as a waistband or button opening. It can also alter the fabric's hand, providing more body.

Interfacings are available in many weights and types. Choosing the most suitable interfacing depends on the weight of your fabric and your desired results. There are woven, knit, and non-woven variants in a multitude of fiber types. Each has its own unique hand, so take a scrap of your fabric to the store with you to help you choose. Use lightweight interfacing for lighter fabrics, and heavyweight interfacing for thicker ones. Featherweight versions are also available for finer fabrics.

There are also fusible interfacings and sew-in interfacings. Fusibles are applied to the fabric with an iron and tend to be stiffer than the sew-in interfacings. Hold and drape your fabric with a variety of interfacings to see which one creates your desired effect.

HOW TO APPLY FUSIBLE INTERFACING

Fusible interfacing is applied to the wrong side of the fabric. Always double-check to make sure the side of the interfacing with the adhesive (usually shiny beads of glue) is facing the fabric. Use a damp press cloth over the interfacing to press (not iron) the interfacing in place with an up-and-down motion. Apply pressure for about 20 seconds, then lift and move the iron, and repeat. Refer to the interfacing manufacturer's instructions to make sure you are using the correct heat setting, and for any specific application tips.

HOW TO ATTACH SEW-IN INTERFACING

Sew-in interfacing should be hand- or machine-basted to the wrong side of the fabric. Pin the interfacing to the fabric, and sew it in place just to the side of the seamline, keeping your stitches within the seam allowance.

Hand Stitches

For fine touches a machine can't handle

Most garment details can be stitched on the machine; however, nothing sews precise details better than a hand needle and thread. Coming up are all the stitches you'll need to complete your own designs and the skirts in this book. Each stitch is worth mastering, and can be used whenever you sew, not only when making garments.

BACK STITCH
This hand stitch can be used to seam garments and it looks very nice from the right side for decorative stitching. For a stronger seam, use shorter stitches.

To start, bring the needle through the fabric from the wrong side to the right side. Then pierce the needle into the fabric to the right of the point where the thread exited the fabric. Bring the needle back up through the fabric to the left of the same thread exit point. Continue.

BASTING STITCH
This temporary stitch is used to hold layers together and for gathering fabric.

To start, bring the needle up through the fabric from the wrong side to the right side. Insert the needle into the fabric again to the left of the original stitch. To continue, bring the needle up to the left of the second stitch. Keep the stitches long, with space between them, so they are easy to remove.

CATCH STITCH
This stitch works well to secure a hem or facing in place because it is invisible from the right side.

Typically, this stitch is worked from left to right, making the stitches feel a little backward at first. To begin, pierce the fabric along the hem or facing from right to left and take a tiny stitch. Then, move about ½" to the right and take a tiny stitch through a few threads of the garment from right to left to make a little X. Repeat.

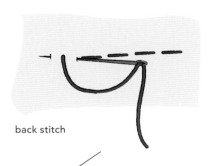
back stitch

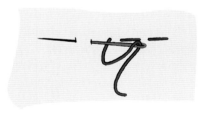
basting stitch

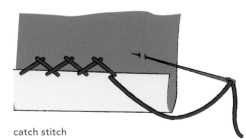
catch stitch

TIP The basting stitch, when taken shorter and with less space between the stitches, is a permanent stitch and is usually referred to as a running stitch.

SLIPSTITCH

Use this stitch to hold a stitched or pressed edge in place.

To start, bring the needle through the folded or pressed edge. Then stitch through a few threads of the garment fabric and pierce the needle back into the fold. Repeat.

SWING TACK

A swing tack is used to secure garment layers together but allows them to move freely, such as a lining and outer garment.

To start, make a small stitch in the outer garment. Leave a 1" length of thread between the two layers and then make a small stitch on the lining. To finish the tack, loop the thread around the exposed thread, knotting each time.

WHIPSTITCH

This stitch is the first hand stitch I learned from my mother when I made my first garment. I used it to secure the bottom edge of a facing, but it also works well to secure hems.

To start, bring the needle up through garment or hem allowance. Then move the needle about ¼" to the side and take a second stitch, making a stitch that wraps around the edge.

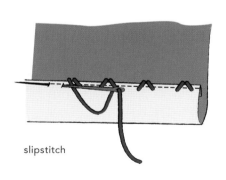

slipstitch

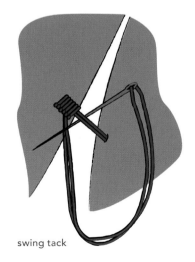

swing tack

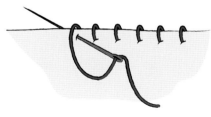

whipstitch

Seams Your Way

Join your pieces with style

Most garment seaming is done with the basic, straight seam, but there are several other types of seams you will enjoy learning. Most seams are stitched with ½"-wide seam allowances, but others require wider seam allowances (such as the flat-felled seam shown on page 32). Be sure to decide the type of seams you want to use before you draft your pattern, and keep the necessary seam allowance width in mind.

CHOOSE YOUR SEAM ALLOWANCE

Seam allowance is the distance between the fabric's raw edge and the sewn seam (or stitch line). It's up to you how much seam allowance you add. You want enough seam allowance to have room to sew, without adding too much bulk.

Most sewing patterns (such as those made by Simplicity, Vogue, and Butterick) include a ⅝"-wide seam allowance. In the garment industry, though, most seams are sewn with a ½"-wide seam allowance, and that's how I've written the instructions for the following seams. You might consider using a smaller seam allowance for seams that will be concealed or turned inside-out, such as those found inside a waistband. For seams like that, I typically use a ¼"-wide seam allowance. If you don't feel comfortable using that small of an allowance, you can always use a larger one when stitching and then trim it down once your seam has been sewn.

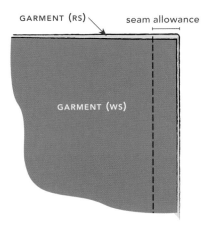

GARMENT (RS)   seam allowance

GARMENT (WS)

TIP Seams into which zippers are sewn sometimes benefit from slightly wider seam allowances, so you might want to add ⅝"-wide allowances to zipper seam edges when drafting a pattern.

RIGHT OR WRONG

The illustrations in this book use a lighter shade for the right side (RS) of the fabric, and a darker shade for the wrong side (WS).

HOW TO SEW DIFFERENT SEAMS

In order to sew any type of garment, you'll want to master how to machine-stitch a variety of seams. The seams listed below are essential to the construction of well-made skirts.

Basic Straight Seam   A basic seam is sewn with the right sides together and raw edges aligned.

1. Use a straight stitch, set to about 8 to 10 stitches per inch. The standard seam allowance is between ½" and ⅝" wide, but you can use any width seam allowance you like.

2. After stitching, press the seam flat, and then press the seam allowances open. To finish, press from the right side of the garment with a press cloth between the garment and the iron.

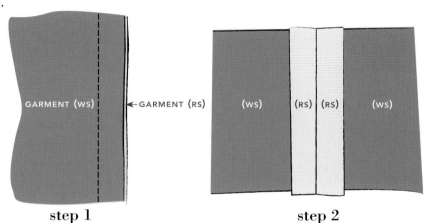

step 1   step 2

French Seam   A French seam is a beautiful, narrow finish without any raw edges, making it a perfect selection for sheer or lace fabrics.

1. To begin, sew the seam with ¼"-wide seam allowances and with the *wrong* sides together and raw edges aligned. Then trim the seam allowance.

2. Next, fold the seam along the stitching line so the wrong sides are together. Sew the seam again, ¼" away from the folded edge.

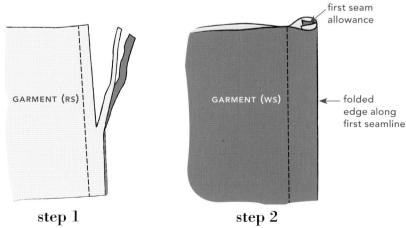

step 1   step 2

Flat-Felled Seam   The flat-felled seam is finished inside and out, and features a decorative topstitch. This seam is frequently used in sportswear and is almost always found on jeans.

1. Start with ¾"-wide seam allowance. Sew the seam with *wrong* sides together and raw edges aligned. Press the seam allowance open and trim one side to ¼".

2. Press the wider seam allowance ¼" to the wrong side and wrap it around the trimmed one. Press it in place.

3. Topstitch the seam allowance along the folded edge through all layers, securing it in place and hiding the raw edges inside.

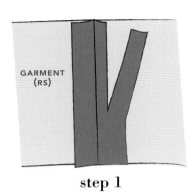
step 1

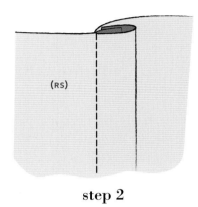
step 2

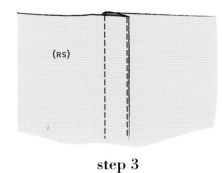
step 3

HOW TO CLEAN FINISH YOUR SEAM EDGES

A well-made garment looks almost as good on the inside as it does on the outside. There are many ways to clean finish the raw edges of seam and hem allowances to minimize raveling and give your skirt a professional looking finish.

Hong Kong Finish   The Hong Kong finished seam starts as a traditional seam, but has finished seam allowance edges, thanks to the application of double-fold bias tape (for more on creating your own bias tape, turn to page 84). You can match the color of the bias tape to your garment or use a contrasting color for added punch on the inside.

1. To begin, stitch a traditional, straight seam with seam allowances at least ½" wide; press the seam open. Press one side of the bias tape open and pin it along the edge of one seam allowance with the right sides together and edges aligned and stitch with ¼"-wide seam.

2. Wrap the bias tape around the edge of the seam allowance. Secure it in place by stitching in the ditch (see the tip on page 69) or just to the inside of the original stitching to catch the bottom of the bias tape in the seam and to completely enclose the raw edge. Stitch only through the bias tape and seam allowance, not the garment.

3. Repeat on the remaining seam allowance to finish.

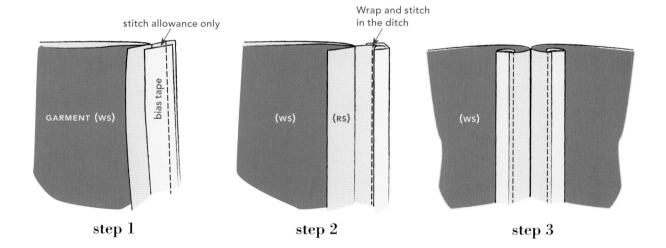

step 1   step 2   step 3

Pinking Shears

This method of finishing your fabric edges is the easiest and quickest. Simply trim your seam allowance edges with pinking shears *after* the seam has been sewn. Do not trim them before you sew the seam. The zigzag cut of the pinking shears will prevent the fabric's edges from fraying during wear and after washing.

Serged or Overlocked Finish

Sergers, or overlock machines, will cut and finish a fabric's edge as it sews. To finish an edge with a serger, sew the seam on the sewing machine first and press the seam allowance normally. Then use the serger to either finish the seam allowances together, or finish them separately to keep the pressed-open look. I typically do not use the serger to sew the initial seam because it cuts as it sews and it creates a stitch that stretches. It's hard to correct sewing accidents once they've been cut and sewn by a serger, so make sure everything is exactly how you want it before you send it through the machine.

Topstitched Edges

Start with a sewn seam that has been pressed open. Then press each seam allowance ⅛" to the wrong side and topstitch each seam allowance edge to secure the raw edge under the stitching.

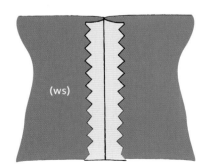

pinking edge finish

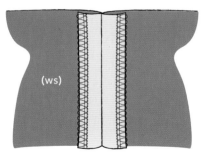

overlock finish

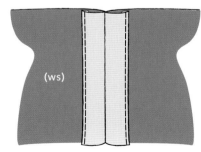

topstitched edge

Zigzag Finish

If you do not own a serger, you can use a zigzag stitch to finish your edges. Start with a seam that has been sewn and pressed open. Then, sewing through the seam allowance only, machine-stitch close to each seam allowance's edge with a zigzag stitch and press to set the stitches. Trim the seam allowance close to the zigzag stitch. The zigzag stitch helps prevent the raw edge from fraying.

Adding the Details
Shape your skirts with ease

Once you've mastered all of the seams and hand stitches, it's time to put those skills to use. Here you'll find all the info you need to get started on those features that, when combined, help you create your skirts.

DARTS

Darts are used to add dimension and shape to flat fabric, and are typically found at the waistline of a skirt (and at the bustline in a full dress).

To sew a dart, fold and pin the garment in the center of the dart with the right sides together and the dart "legs" aligned. Begin sewing at the garment raw edge and finish by sewing straight along the dart leg and off the dart point. Hand knot the thread ends or run the thread for a couple of stitches beyond the dart point to let the threads twist.

Press the stitched dart flat to set the stitches, but take care not to press a crease beyond the dart point. Then, working on a tailor's ham (see page 18), press the dart toward either the center back or center front to set the garment's curve. To finish, press the dart again from the right side using a press cloth between the garment and the iron.

CORNERS

Garment details, such as sharp corners, create an interesting predicament. When the fabric pieces are placed right sides together, their raw edges don't line up. This will come up in the Piece Gathering Skirt on page 185, when you sew in the gathered panel.

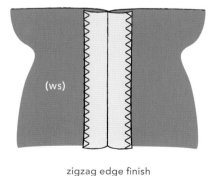

zigzag edge finish

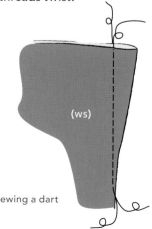

sewing a dart

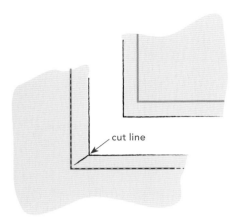

cut line

step 1

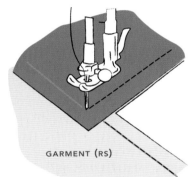

GARMENT (RS)

step 2

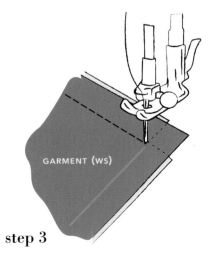

GARMENT (WS)

step 3

1. To sew these edges together, first mark their seamlines with a temporary fabric marker. To prevent tearing and stretching, stitch just inside the seamline, pivoting at the corner (this is called staystitching). Then clip into the inside corner piece as shown, being careful not to cut through the marked seamline.

2. Pin the pieces with the right sides together and raw edges aligned. Stitch one long edge up to the corner. With the needle still in the fabric, lift the presser foot.

3. Pivot the fabric, and gently pull the clipped piece underneath to match the top layer. The clip in the seam allowance should open up, allowing you to align the pieces with ease. Lower the presser foot and complete the seam.

CURVES

Like sharp corners, curved seams do not match up perfectly when they are positioned with the right sides together.

1. Mark the seamlines directly on both garment pieces with a temporary fabric marker. To prevent tearing and stretching, stitch just inside the seamline close to the curve (this is called staystitching).

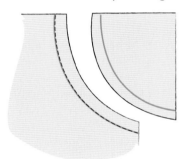

2. Cut tiny notches into the seam allowance of the concave piece, taking care not to cut through the marked seamline. These notches will allow the curve to spread and fit the opposing piece better.

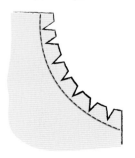

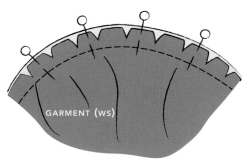

GARMENT (WS)

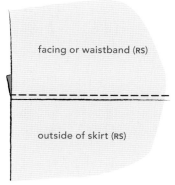

facing or waistband (RS)

outside of skirt (RS)

understitching

it to penetrate several layers of fabric. The Twiggy Skirt (see page 123) is an example of a skirt top-stitched this way with contrasting thread.

EDGESTITCHING

Edgestitching is created by sewing close to a garment edge or fold, typically no more than ⅛" away.

UNDERSTITCHING

Understitching is a simple extra step that goes a long way toward helping your garment look its best from the outside. It may seem like an annoying extra step, but trust me; it is well worth the time and effort. Typically done on facing and waistband seams to prevent the seamline from rolling to the right side, understitching holds the facing (or other interior piece) in place.

To understitch, machine-stitch the seam as usual and then press the seam allowance toward the facing (or the piece that is being turned inside the garment). Then, edgestitch the seam allowance in place just inside the seamline. You'll be amazed at how easily the seamline then turns under, without rolling to the garment's right side.

3. Spread the seam allowance of the concave piece to match the convex piece, pinning them together with several pins. Machine-stitch the seam as usual, taking care not to stitch any of the puckers.

TOPSTITCHING

Topstitching is sewn from the right side of the garment and is meant to be visible on the finished garment. Regular sewing thread is used for most topstitched details, but for decorative work, topstitching thread stands out more. If you use topstitching thread, switch your machine setting to a longer stitch length (about 3.5 mm) and use a topstitching needle. This special needle has a larger eye to accommodate the thicker thread, and is stronger and sharper to enable

GATHERING

Gathering can be used to create ruffles or ruched details. It's really easy to do using a machine basting stitch. To start, stitch one or two basting stitches inside the seam allowance along the edge you'd like to gather. Backstitch at one end and leave the other end of the thread tails long.

To gather the edge, pull the bobbin thread's long tail. Push the fabric along the thread and gather it to your desired length and fullness.

Closing Time
Sew great-looking closures

Garment closures can simply be utilitarian or a design element — it's up to you. There are plenty of options available, including buttons, snaps, and zippers. Experiment with different closures to decide which works best for your style.

BUTTONHOLES

Refer to your owner's manual for making machine-stitched button-holes. The standard buttonhole with bar tacks at each end can be placed horizontally or vertically, depending on the design of the skirt. To determine the button-hole length, add ⅛" to the width of the button. Make a practice buttonhole on scrap fabric before making one on your project.

BUTTONS

With all of the different buttons available today, it's easy to create a closure that becomes a stylish detail instead of a simple closure.

Sew-Through Buttons

When it comes to sew-through buttons, how you stitch them is really up to you. With four-hole buttons, you can make an X with the thread or run the stitches from side to side.

1. Start sewing from the right side of the garment by taking a small stitch through a few garment threads, at the button location.

2. Bring the needle up through one hole in the button and place a toothpick over the button.

3. Sew down through the next hole and through the garment.

4. Repeat multiple times to secure the button in place. Sewing over the toothpick creates a "shank" that allows the garment's layers to fit comfortably underneath the button.

5. To finish, remove the tooth-pick, pull the button up from the fabric gently, and wrap the thread around the "thread shank" underneath the button a few times. Then stitch through the garment again and knot off the thread underneath the button.

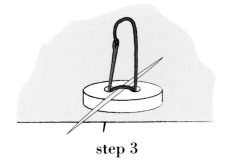

step 3

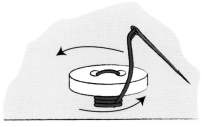

step 5

Shank Buttons

A shank button has a loop underneath it for sewing through and to hold the button away from the fabric. To sew a shank button:

1. Start by knotting your thread and make a stitch through the fabric at the button location on the garment's right side.

2. Thread the needle through the button's shank.

3. Make a small stitch at the button placement on the garment and pull the thread taut.

4. Repeat to sew through the button shank several times.

5. To finish, make a stitch through the garment and knot off the thread.

HOOKS AND EYES

Hooks and eyes are typically positioned above zippers, and on waistbands, to help hold skirts closed.

- For garment edges that overlap, pin the garment closed and mark where you want to sew on the hook and eye with a temporary fabric marker.

- For garment edges that meet, pin the garment closed and mark the position of the hook 1/16" from the garment edge and the eye so that it extends just beyond the garment edge.

Regardless of positioning, sew the hooks and eyes by taking stitches inside each of the loops and knotting after each stitch.

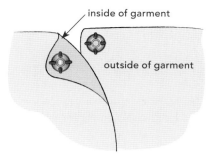

inside of garment

outside of garment

SNAPS

Snaps are sold in two pieces that fit together perfectly. To sew a snap to your skirt, try it on and mark where you want the snap to go. Make sure you mark where each side of the snap will be placed. Then, sew each snap to the garment, taking multiple stitches through each hole, and knotting after each stitch.

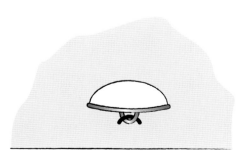

shank button

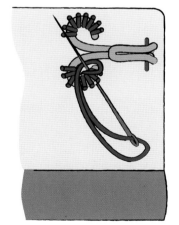
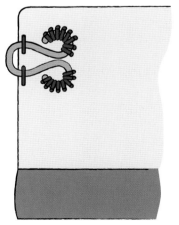

sewing hook and eye

ZIPPERS

Zippers may look daunting at first, but don't fret. With a few tricks up your sleeve and a zipper presser foot, they're really simple to sew. When choosing the most appropriate zipper application, keep your design in mind. Each of these applications looks a little different from the outside because some have visible topstitching and others don't. Typically in skirts, zippers are located on the left side or the center back. Choose the location based on your desired look.

Centered Application

A centered zipper application is most common and has stitching visible on the right side of the garment. A ½" or ⅝"-wide seam allowance is adequate.

1. Machine-baste the seam where the zipper will go closed. Stitch the remainder of the seam closed with a shorter, permanent stitch length, backstitching first at the bottom of the zipper seam. Press the seam allowance open.

2. Mark stitching lines on the right side of the garment with a temporary fabric marker. Mark the lines ¼" away from each side of the seamline and across the seam just below the location of the bottom of the zipper.

3. Turn the garment wrong side up and center the zipper, right side down over the seamline. Position the top of the zipper ½" to ⅝" below the top edge of the skirt. Secure the zipper in place with hand basting stitches or double-sided basting tape.

4. Install the zipper foot and with the garment right side up machine-stitch along the marked lines. Pick open the basted seam with a seam ripper to expose the center of the zipper.

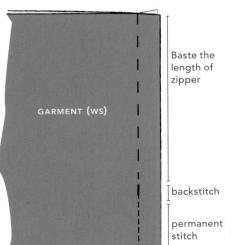

GARMENT (WS)

Baste the length of zipper

backstitch

permanent stitch

step 1

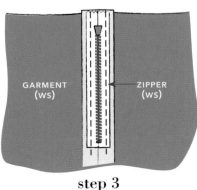

GARMENT (RS)

step 2

GARMENT (WS)　ZIPPER (WS)

step 3

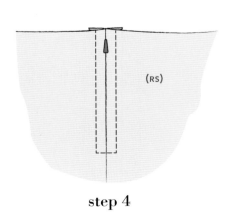

(RS)

step 4

Invisible Application

An invisible zipper is not visible from the right side; all you see is the seam. There are special presser feet made for installing invisible zippers, available at most fabric stores. The special foot isn't absolutely necessary to install this zipper, but it does make the job incredibly easier. The coils of an invisible zipper curl back on themselves, so the zipper needs to be pressed before it's sewn in place: Press the coils open along each zipper tape with low heat, being careful to not melt the coils as you press. This zipper is installed in an unstitched seam.

1. With the zipper open, pin one side of the zipper to the garment opening with the right sides together and the zipper coils aligned with the seamline. Install the invisible zipper foot and machine-stitch the zipper tape in place.

2. Stitch the remaining zipper tape to the remaining garment opening with the right sides together as in the previous step.

3. Install the standard presser foot. To finish, close the zipper and from the wrong side, backstitch and then machine-stitch the rest of the garment opening closed, from the bottom of the zipper to the hemline. Fold the bottom end of the zipper out of the way of the stitching.

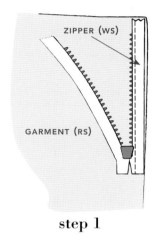

ZIPPER (WS)

GARMENT (RS)

step 1

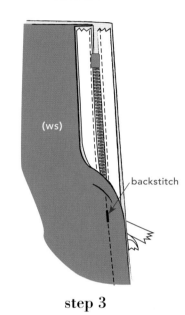

(ws)

backstitch

step 3

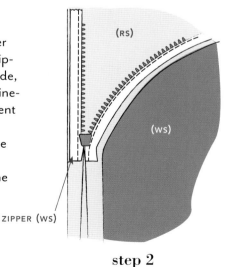

(RS)

(ws)

ZIPPER (WS)

step 2

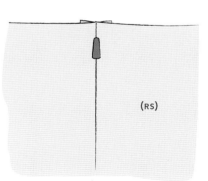

(RS)

finished zipper

Lapped Application

A lapped zipper application uses a traditional zipper; however, the zipper is hidden with a lap of fabric that is topstitched in place. For directional purposes, this zipper is being applied in a center-back seam.

1. Machine-stitch the garment opening below the zipper opening with the right sides together, starting with a backstitch. On the right side, mark the seam allowances on the remaining garment opening with a temporary fabric marker.

2. Press the right seam allowance ⅛" to the wrong side, just inside the marked seamline. Press the left seam allowance to the wrong side along the marked seamline.

3. Install the zipper foot. Pin the closed zipper along the folded right side of the garment opening. Edgestitch close to the zipper teeth/coils.

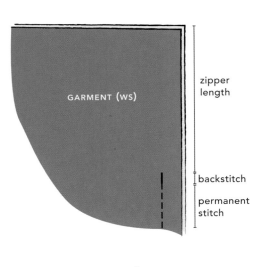

step 1

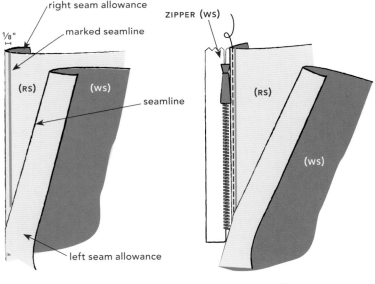

step 2

step 3

4. Pin the garment closed so that the left folded edge creates a lap and the marked seamlines are aligned.

5. Topstitch the zipper in place, ½" to ⅝" away from the lapped fold, pivoting across the bottom of the zipper. Backstitch or pull the top thread to the wrong side and knot the threads at the bottom edge of the zipper.

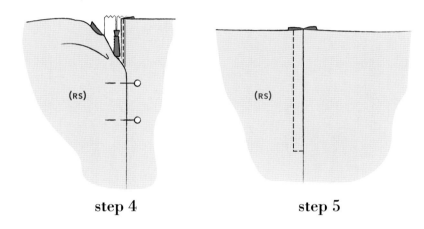

step 4   step 5

TIP It's easier to stitch straight along the outside of a lapped zipper if you mark the stitch line with a temporary fabric marker before sewing.

Exposed Zipper Application

An exposed zipper application displays the zipper on the right side of the garment. There are zippers available with satin tape, metallic tape, and even multicolored teeth. Feature these truly unique notions with this easy application technique. If your fabric is lightweight, fuse a strip of interfacing to the wrong side of the zipper opening.

1. On the right side of each of the garment pieces being joined, baste ⅛" to the left of the seamline of the zipper opening. Baste across the bottom as well. Then pin the two garment pieces with the right sides together and raw edges aligned. Machine-stitch the seam beneath the zipper opening. Mark a diagonal line from the corner at the bottom of the basted zipper opening to the side edges as shown.

2. Clip the seam allowances up to (but not through) the basting stitches at the bottom of the zipper on the marked line. Press the seam allowances to the right side along the basting stitches.

3. Press the bottom edge of the zipper to the wrong side. With the zipper facing up, pin it in place over the opening and on the right side of the garment. Hand-baste the zipper in place along each side of the zipper tape.

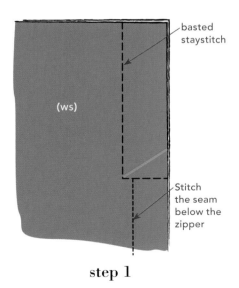

basted staystitch

(ws)

Stitch the seam below the zipper

step 1

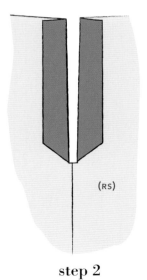

(RS)

step 2

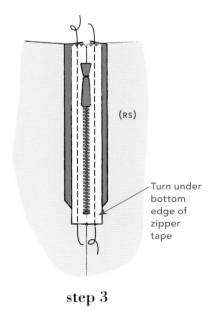

(RS)

Turn under bottom edge of zipper tape

step 3

4. Topstitch the zipper in place: on one side of the zipper teeth, machine-stitch from the top of the zipper along the outside edge of the zipper tape; pivot and stitch across the bottom of the tape, stopping short of the teeth; pivot again and stitch up the same side of the zipper tape to the top edge. Repeat on the opposite side of the zipper teeth.

Make sure the stitches go through both the zipper tape and the fabric so that the zipper is secured in place. Remove the hand basting, and press, using a press cloth.

The Bottom Line

Master hems for a pro finish

The hem is typically the last thing you sew on your garment, but it needs to be considered long before you make the first stitch. Select the most appropriate hem treatment based on your fabric and garment silhouette, then allow for enough fabric at the bottom when you draft the skirt.

To figure out where to place the hem once you've sewn your skirt, simply try it on and let the fabric hang on your body. Then mark on the skirt where you would like the hem to end. You can do this with any temporary fabric marker, or by simply placing a pin at the desired hem level. Then, take off the skirt and pin up the hem allowance along the desired finished edge. Make sure you measure all the way around the skirt to make the hem consistent and even. Then try on the skirt again to double-check the length. Make sure the hem is parallel to the ground all the way around (if you want it that way, of course).

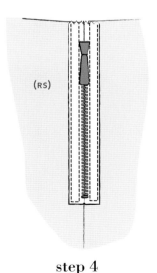

(RS)

step 4

Choose Your Hem Allowance

TYPE OF SKIRT	HEM WIDTH
Basic straight skirt	2" to 2½"
Flared (A-line) skirt	½" to 1"
Full, gathered skirt	½" to 1½"
Circular or bias cut skirt	⅜" to ¾"
Heavy fabric	2" to 2½"
Sheer fabric	½" to ⅝"

HEMMING HEAVYWEIGHT FABRICS

For thicker fabrics, such as heavy wools, cashmeres, and fleeces, a little extra hem support is needed.

- For patternmaking, allow 2" to 2½" for the hem allowance. Clean finish the raw edge (see pages 33–35).

For straight silhouettes, turn up the entire hem allowance and press. Partially fold the hem allowance back down and hand-sew it in place about 1" above the hemline with a catch stitch (see page 28). Then, fold the top part of the hem back up and catch-stitch along the hem allowance edge.

TOPSTITCHED HEM

The topstitched hem is the quickest hemline to sew. However, it leaves a line of stitching on the garment's right side, so keep that in mind as you're designing.

- For patternmaking, allow a 2" to 2½"-wide hem allowance. You don't need to clean finish the raw edge because it is enclosed in the hem.

Press the raw edge ½" to the wrong side. Then, turn and press the hem 1½" to 2" to the wrong side along the hemline. Topstitch the hem allowance in place along the inner fold.

A narrower version of this double-fold hem is frequently used to finish off other edges, such as the outside edge of a wrap skirt. In that case, press under the raw edge ½" to the wrong side, then press under another ½", then topstitch. Occasionally the project instructions will call for a ¼" double-fold hem.

note

- -

Turning the raw edge on heavyweight fabric would make the hem too bulky. Usually, a catch stitch will keep a raw edge from raveling, but if you like, you can zigzag or serge this edge before doing the catch stitch.

- -

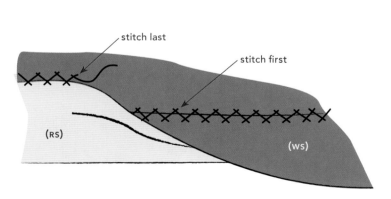

stitch last

stitch first

(RS)

(WS)

hemming heavyweight fabrics

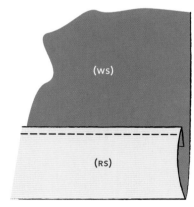

(WS)

(RS)

topstitched hem

HEMMING FULL SILHOUETTES

Unfortunately, a wide hem on a full skirt won't turn under and press flat because the hem allowance is wider than the garment.

- For patternmaking, allow a ¾" to 1½"-wide hem allowance.

For light- to medium-weight fabrics, ease the hem edge by stitching one row of gathering stitches and pulling the stitches slightly. Once the hem edge fits the inside of the garment, stitch hem lace or hem tape to the edge (if the fabric doesn't ravel, you can leave the hem edge unfinished). Once the hem allowance has been eased, press it in place. Machine-topstitch or hand-sew it in place.

Alternatively, for heavier fabrics, you can cut slashes into the hemline and overlap them to reduce the bulk. If the fabric ravels, you can use a fray-stopper product to stop the raveling, or you can finish the edges with pinking shears.

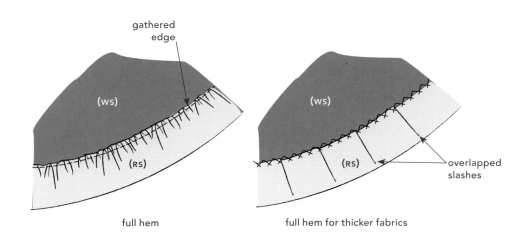

gathered edge

(ws)

(RS)

full hem

(ws)

(RS)

overlapped slashes

full hem for thicker fabrics

NARROW HEM

I love this hem treatment for fine fabrics and full silhouettes, on fabrics such as batiste, chiffon, charmeuse, and other lightweight materials.

- For patternmaking, allow a ⅝"-wide hem allowance.

There is no need to clean finish the raw edge, as it will be enclosed in the hem. To stitch a narrow hem:

1. Stitch around the hem edge ⅜" from the raw edge. Press the raw edge to the wrong side along the stitch line and stitch again just inside the fold.

2. Trim the hem allowance close to the stitching. Then roll the hem allowance to the wrong side again, hiding the raw edge. Edgestitch the hem in place.

MACHINE-STITCHED BLIND HEM

A blind hem is invisible on the right side of the garment as long as the thread color blends well with the fabric. To stitch, first consult your sewing machine manual to determine the proper presser foot, install the right presser foot, and select the "blind hem" stitch. Usually it looks like a straight stitch that kicks out to the side every five stitches or so.

- For patternmaking, allow a hem allowance that is at least 1½" wide.

Clean finish the raw edge as desired. To start:

1. Fold the desired hem allowance to the wrong side and pin it in place.

2. Fold the garment back, exposing the hem allowance's raw edge, as shown in the diagram.

3. Select a blind stitch on your machine, and stitch along the hem allowance and use the presser foot to guide the stitch so that when the stitch extends to the left, it catches the garment.

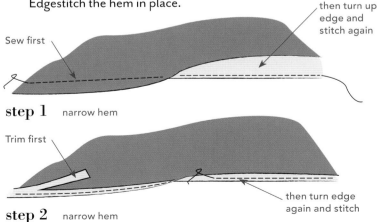

Sew first

then turn up edge and stitch again

step 1   narrow hem

Trim first

then turn edge again and stitch

step 2   narrow hem

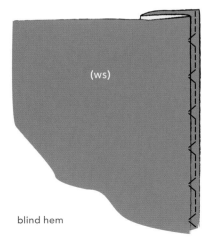

(ws)

blind hem

FACED HEM

A faced hem works well on a curved or shaped hemline. I used it on the asymmetrical hemline on page 102 because the skirt has a dramatic curve across the bottom. You can use fabric or a wide strip of bias tape for the facing. (For help on creating your own bias tape, turn to page 84.)

- For patternmaking, allow regular seam allowance, but you will need to draft the facing (page 104, step 7).

1. Clean finish the top edge of the facing using your favorite method. Pin the facing to the garment at the hem edge with right sides together and raw edges aligned, and stitch.

2. Press the seam allowance toward the facing and under-stitch (page 37) in place. Then press the facing to the wrong side. To secure the top edge of the facing to the skirt, topstitch it in place, or hand-sew (see hand stitches on pages 28–29) so the stitches are invisible from the right side.

HAND-SEWN HEM

For an invisible finish from the garment's right side, there are several hand stitches that will help you tame unruly fabrics and look great both inside and out. I like to use the slipstitch (page 29), catch stitch (page 28), or whip-stitch (page 29) when finishing hems by hand.

To hand-sew a hem, simply press the desired width hem allowance to the wrong side. Then clean finish the raw edge using your favorite method. Pin the hem in place (if you have to ease it, use lots of pins) and hand-sew, taking care to only stitch through one or two garment threads.

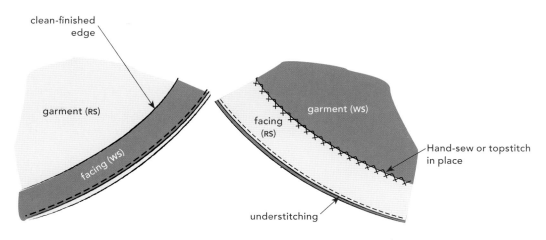

clean-finished edge

garment (RS)

facing (WS)

step 1

facing (RS)

garment (WS)

Hand-sew or topstitch in place

understitching

step 2

PADDED HEM

A padded hemline makes a soft edge on thicker fabrics, especially those with nap, such as velvet or mohair.

- For patternmaking, allow a 2" to 2½"-wide hem allowance. Clean finish the raw edge as desired.

1. For padding, cut a strip of flannel fabric along the bias (page 25) the same width as the hem allowance. Position the bias strip about ¾" from the garment's raw edge. Secure the edges of the flannel in place with a catch stitch.

2. Turn up the hem allowance along the hemline. The bias strip should be exposed above the hem allowance for ¾". Secure the hem allowance in place with a catch stitch (page 28), taking care to only sew through the padding.

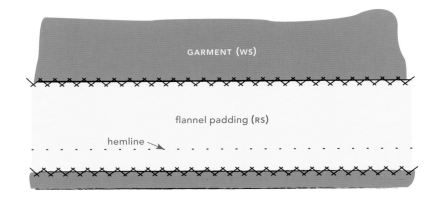

GARMENT (WS)

flannel padding (RS)

hemline →

step 1

GARMENT (WS)

flannel padding (RS)

hem allowance (RS)

Sew hem to padding only

step 2

REINFORCED HEM

A reinforced hem, such as the one found in the Jazz Age Skirt (trumpet silhouette) on page 201, adds shape and support to a hemline. This hem is ideal for flared and A-line silhouettes. Typically, horsehair braid — a stiff, mesh-like material available in various widths — is sewn into the hemline. It once was made from actual horsehair, but today it's completely synthetic.

- For patternmaking, allow a hem allowance slightly wider than the width of the horsehair braid. Do not finish the raw edge; it will be hidden by horsehair.

For wider horsehair braids, make sure you add a hem allowance to your pattern that is wider than the braid. Gently pull the gathering cord found on the edge of the braid to ease it slightly. Then position the braid with the non-corded edge along the hemline. Hand-sew the braid in place along the bottom edge with a catch stitch or whipstitch. Then, press the hem allowance to the wrong side, turn under the raw edge, and catch-stitch it in place, hiding the braid.

For narrow horsehair braids:

1. Stitch it to the garment with right sides together along the hemline.

2. Fold and press the braid to the garment's inside and catch-stitch it in place.

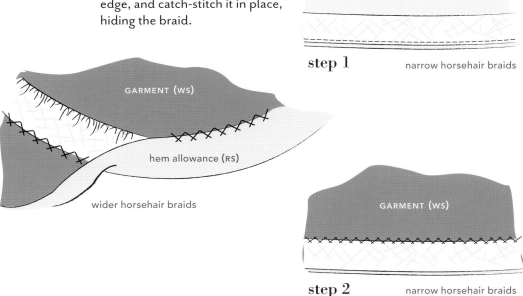

GARMENT (WS)

hem allowance (RS)

wider horsehair braids

GARMENT (RS)

step 1   narrow horsehair braids

GARMENT (WS)

step 2   narrow horsehair braids

chapter 3

DRAFT YOUR OWN CUSTOM PATTERNS

Now that you've stocked up on everything you need to get started and reviewed basic sewing instructions, let the designing begin! In this chapter, you'll see how easy it is to draft a customized master pattern that you can use to develop any of the designs found in this book, plus any other variation you can think of. All you need to get started are accurate body measurements (see next page). Nothing is more flattering than a garment made using your own dimensions. Plus, you'll have the satisfaction of knowing that you made the entire thing yourself.

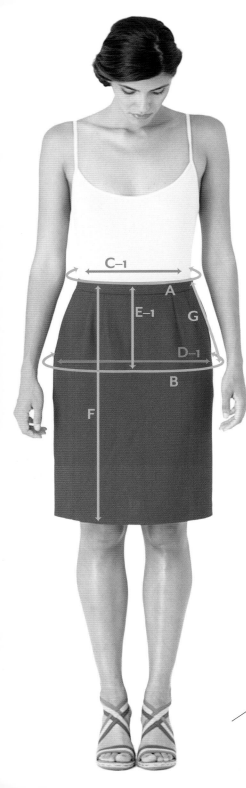

Body Measurements

Great patterns start with accurate measurements

One of the greatest things about creating your own clothes is getting a personalized fit, and that starts with accurate measurements. Make sure you have a good tape measure, straight pins, and a body-hugging outfit. It's difficult to take good measurements if you are wearing bulky clothing because the tape measure needs to wrap rather snugly against your body (but not so tight that it's uncomfortable or alters your size).

Having a friend help you is easier than taking your own measurements, but as long as you have a mirror you can take them yourself. Make sure you stand naturally with your weight evenly distributed on both feet. And, when you are taking width-wise measurements, make sure the measuring tape is parallel to the floor. A slight slant of the tape can throw off the measurement and cause fitting problems later.

Prepare to take and record all the measurements described. Keep them in a safe place so you can refer to them while drafting your designs. I have a notebook in my work area where my measurements live, so I can refer to them for each new project.

TIP You can tie ribbons around your true waist and hips to mark them for future measurements.

BODY WIDTH MEASUREMENTS

Total true-waist circumference (A). Your true waist is probably higher than you think. It is usually the narrowest part of your body, slightly above your belly button. Your master pattern (or sloper) will be drafted up to this point. Don't worry; you'll learn how to lower (and raise) the waistline if you want to (page 65). While you have the measuring tape around your body, use straight pins or a temporary fabric marker to mark your true waistline at the center-front, center-back, and side seams of your body-hugging garment. This will help you remember where you measured your true waist when it's time to take length measurements.

Front waist (C–1). Measure your front waist from side seam to side seam across the front of your body.

Back waist (C–2). Measure your back waist from side seam to side seam across the back of your body (not shown).

Total hip circumference (B). Your hip circumference measurement is taken around the fullest part of your hips, between 7" and 9" below your true waist. Make sure the tape is parallel to the floor all the way around your body and mark your hipline at the center-front, center-back, and side seams with a pin or a temporary fabric marker. This will help you remember where you measured your hip circumference so you can take accurate length measurements later.

Front hip (D–1). Measure your front hips from side seam to side seam across the front of your body.

Back hip (D–2). Measure your back hips from side seam to side seam across the back of your body (not shown).

BODY LENGTH MEASUREMENTS

Front waist to hip (E–1). This is the distance from your true waist to your hips along your center front.

Back waist to hip (E–2). This is the distance from your true waist to your hips along your center back (not shown).

Side waist to hips (G). This is the distance from your true waist to your hips along your side seam.

Waist to knee (F). This is the distance from your true waist to the top of your knee. Your master skirt pattern (sloper) will be drafted to your knee, but it is easy to change the skirt length to suit your designs.

note

When added together, your front and back waist should equal your total true waist. The same goes for your hip measurements. Double-check them to make sure they are accurate. If they are terribly off, you are probably reaching too far (or not far enough) over the sides when you are taking the front and back measurements. If you're having trouble, you can always mark with straight pins where you start and stop each measurement at the sides.

Draft a Customized Skirt Sloper

The building block for your own designs

In fashion design, the pattern you start with is called a sloper, or block pattern. It is made to fit you without any flare at the hem and it runs the length of your body from your true waist to the top of your knee.

You will use your sloper as the starting point for all the designs in this book. If you use the sloper to sew a skirt exactly as you draft it, without any design changes, you'll create a straight or pencil skirt.

It is important to understand the concept of "ease." Because your body is dimensional and patterns are flat, you need to add wearing ease or darts to your skirt patterns to duplicate your body shape. You draft a basic sloper from your measurements and then use ease or darts to create shape and design.

HOW TO MAKE YOUR PERSONALIZED SLOPER

The skirt pattern is drafted by drawing half of the skirt front and half of the skirt back. If you're new to sewing with patterns, take a look at the photograph on page 63 so you can see what you're working toward. Don't worry if your slopers don't match the diagrams exactly; everyone's skirt pattern looks slightly different due to different measurements.

For the sloper, you will draft 1"-wide darts in the back and ½"-wide darts in the front. These are fairly standard widths, but can be adjusted as needed.

1. *Draw two boxes.*

Draw two boxes next to each other using the measurements as indicated in the illustration. One box is half of the skirt front and the other box is half of the skirt back. I like to draw the center line (which becomes the side seam) and work outward, but you can draw your lines any way you'd like. Plot the measurements on the next page, one line at a time. Each key measurement is color-coded in the illustrations.

½ of **back hip (D–2)** measurement + ½" for ease _____

½ of **front hip (D–1)** measurement + ½" for ease _____

Front waist to hip (E–1) _____

Front waist to knee (F) _____

Back waist to hip (E–2) _____

On the center back, measure from the hipline up and add a hash mark to indicate this measurement. This mark can be above or below the top (waist) line, depending on your measurements.

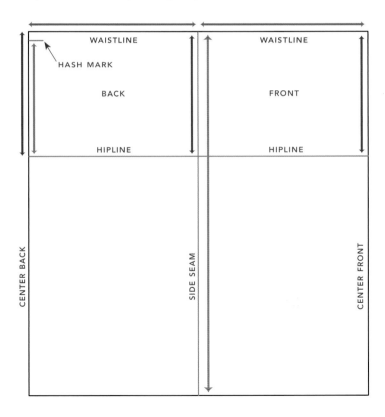

Ease is extra room built into the pattern to allow for comfort and movement.

Darts in skirts are typically triangular in shape and located at the waistline. Drafting darts into your pattern allows your garment to follow the contours and curves of your body. The basic skirt sloper has two darts on each side, in both the front and back, for a total of eight darts in the finished skirt.

note

If you are athletic- or straight-shaped, with less than a 7" difference in circumference between your waist and hips, you might only need one dart on your front and back patterns. Don't worry; this isn't incorrect. It just means that you are slightly less curvy than standard measurements. See page 64 for how to draft one dart instead of two.

2. *Draft the waistline and side seams.*

½ of **back waist** (C–2) + 2¼" (for two 1" darts + ease) _____
Measure this distance from the center back along the top line and make a hash mark. If this measurement goes beyond your side seam don't worry; in that case you should draft one dart instead of two (add 1¼" instead of 2¼").

½ of **front waist** (C–1) + 1¼" (for two ½" darts + ease) _____
Measure this distance from the center front along the top line and make a hash mark. If this measurement goes beyond your side seam, don't worry; draft one dart instead of two (add ¾" instead of 1¼").

side waist to hips (G) _____
Use your hip curve ruler to draw in the new curved side seams, starting 2" above the hipline and going upward to (and possibly through) the hash mark. Typically this curved line will reach slightly above the top edge of the box.

Draw in the new waistline by using your curve to join the new side-seam hash marks to the center front and center back. For the center back, make sure to draw the curve to the hash mark, not just to the top of the box.

TIP Make sure to draft square corners (90-degree angles) at each side seam and at the center front and center back. See Drafting Corners on the opposite page.

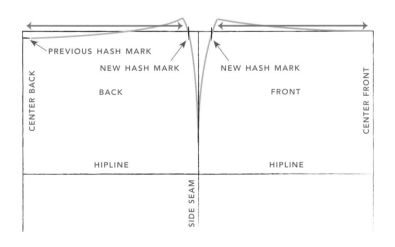

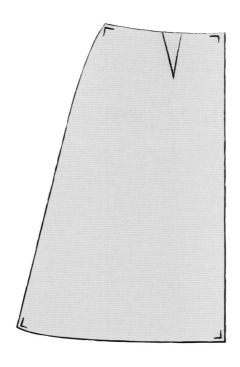

DRAFTING CORNERS

When drafting a pattern, there are a few corners that should always be right angles to ensure they look straight on your body. Those corners on a skirt are typically the top and bottom edge of both the center front and center back, and the top and bottom corners of each side seam.

To do this, simply align the corner of your straight ruler with the skirt's vertical line. Then trace the right angle from ruler's adjoining edge for ¼". Blend this corner into the curved skirt edge.

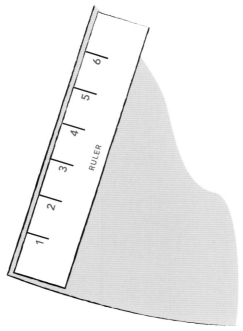

3. Plot the darts.

Draw the first registration line for the back dart 2¾" in from the center back. Draw the second line for that first dart 1" away from the first line.

Draw the first registration line for the front dart 3" in from the center front. Draw the second line for that first dart ½" away from the first line.

Draw lines for the second darts in both the front and back, 1¼" away from the first. (If you are very curvy, space your back darts 1½" apart.) Draw the second lines for the second darts ½" away from the first line for the front dart and 1" away from the first line for the back dart.

4. Draft the darts.

Draw a registration line through the center of each dart and measure down that line from the top edge of the skirt (not the box) as follows: 5½" for the back dart closest to the center back and 3½" for all the other darts. Draw the dart legs.

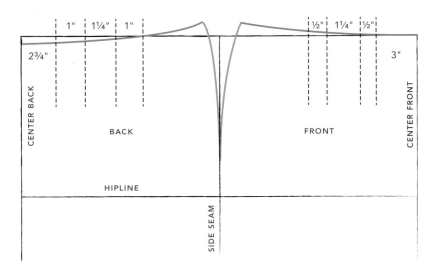

step 3

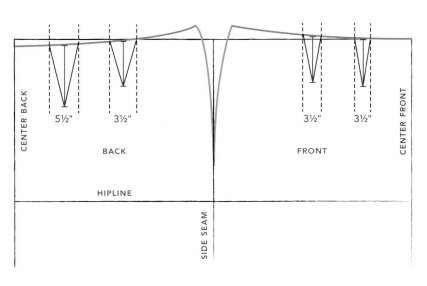

step 4

5. True up the top edges of the darts.

a) Once the darts are drafted, you'll need to true them up. This is so the top edge of the skirt will be even once the darts are sewn and pressed in the correct direction.

b) To true a dart, fold the paper along the dart markings just as you would if you were working with the fabric version. Crease the paper along the dart leg and the center line, and then fold the dart's excess toward the center of the garment. If the markings for the top of the skirt don't match, blend them so they align perfectly (shown in red).

Trim across the top edge of the folded dart so it is even across the top edge of the sloper. When you unfold the pattern, there should be a slight peak at the center of the dart.

6. Test the sloper.
Before you use your sloper to design a skirt, you need to test that it fits your body. Refer to Making a Test Skirt (Muslin) on the next page and then transfer any fit changes from the marked test skirt to the slopers.

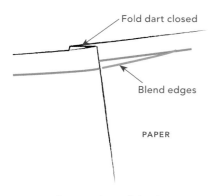

Fold dart closed

Blend edges

PAPER

True up the top edges of the darts, part 1

trued darts usually have slight peak

step 5a

step 5b

MAKING A TEST SKIRT (MUSLIN)

A test skirt made from a sloper is often called a muslin, because slopers are traditionally made from this unbleached, inexpensive fabric. Here's how you make one.

1. Fold your fabric along the lengthwise grain, so the fold is parallel to the selvages. Pin the slopers to the fabric with both the center front and the center back positioned on the fabric fold (so when you unfold the fabric you have a whole fabric front and a whole fabric back). Transfer all the markings (see page 72) from the slopers to your fabric, including the center front and back, hiplines, and dart legs. Add a 1"-wide seam allowance to the side seams, and the top and bottom edges. Make sure to draw all of the seamlines onto your fabric as well.

note

You add wider than usual seam allowance in case you want to let out the seams for better fit.

2. Cut out your skirt front and back from the fabric.

3. Machine-stitch the darts (see page 35) and one side seam of your skirt; partially stitch the other side seam but leave the top open enough that you can get it on and off. In an actual skirt, the seam would be finished with a zipper, but that isn't necessary on a test skirt.

note

I like to assemble the entire muslin using temporary basting stitches so I can remove them quickly during fitting. I also like to use contrasting thread so the stitches are easily visible.

4. Try on the skirt and pin the side seam closed. Look for the following:

- Double-check that there aren't pull lines across your hips (indicating that the skirt is too small), or sagging fabric (indicating that it is too large).
- If the skirt is too tight, let out the side seams using a seam ripper, and pin the new side seam to fit.
- If the skirt is too loose, pin out the excess. Make sure there are no wrinkles in the skirt.
- Make sure the skirt doesn't gape at the waist and is contoured to fit your shape, and that the top edge of the skirt stays parallel to the floor. If necessary, mark a new waistline.
- The center-front and center-back marked lines should align with the center of your body. Each dart should end just shy of your fullest parts.

TIP Once you have perfected the fit of your sloper, you will use it repeatedly, putting it through plenty of wear and tear. Prolong the life of your sloper by tracing it onto and then cutting it from a sturdy paper such as oak tag or gridded plastic.

- A well-fitted skirt should have a hipline that runs straight across the body, parallel to the floor.
- Adjust the skirt length if desired. Double-check that the hemline is straight and the center front and back fall correctly.

5. Mark any new seamlines with a marker or pencil right on the fabric. Use a different color than the one you used to mark the original lines.

6. Once all of the changes have been marked, resew the muslin following the new markings and using a basting stitch to double-check the fit.

One of the greatest perks of custom-made clothes is perfect fit, so really take your time with this. This sloper will be the foundation for all of your future designs and you want them to fit perfectly. Once you're happy with the fit, transfer all of the changes to the paper pattern, omitting all seam and hem allowances.

Basic Sloper Design Variations

Get started with designing

There are a few standard design variations that you will use repeatedly to create the skirt projects in this book. Once you master these, including drafting a waistband to finish the top edge of your skirt, you'll be able to move on to more unique and creative designing.

DRAFT A ONE-DART SLOPER

Depending on your design, you may want to have only one dart instead of two on each sloper (total of two darts in the front and two in the back). The process is very simple, and can be completed quickly and easily as illustrated below.

1. Mark the center between both darts along the top edge on both the skirt front and back. Draw a line from this mark that is parallel to the center front equal and the same length as the darts.

2. Measure the width of the outer dart (x) on the skirt front sloper. Divide this in half and shave that amount off the side seam. Draw a new central dart on the line you drew in step 1. The width of the new dart should be half the amount of the outer dart (x) + the width of the inner dart (y). Make the length of the new dart about ¼" longer than the old inside dart.

Example: If you drafted the standard size darts for your sloper, your front darts are both ½" wide. Therefore you will shave ¼" off the side seam and draft a new ¾"-wide dart.

3. Repeat steps 1 and 2 on the back sloper.

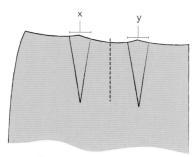

step 1

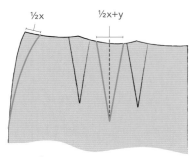

step 2

TIP It's a good idea to make design variations on a *copy* of your perfect fitting sloper, not the original, so you always have a good, clean copy of the sloper to design from. Trace the sloper on drafting paper and make all your design changes to the copy.

DRAFT A LOWER WAISTLINE

Your sloper was drafted with the waist at your true waist, which is not where most ready-to-wear clothing sits today. To adjust your waistline to sit lower than your true waist, put on a skirt or pants that come to the right place, and use that as a guide for measuring your body from your true waist to the top of the waistline.

Apply that measurement to both slopers by measuring down from and across the top edge. Draw in the new waistlines parallel to the original, and cut off the excess. That's it! You've now lowered your sloper's waistline and can draft a waistband or facing to fit this new waist edge. Now, that wasn't so hard, was it?

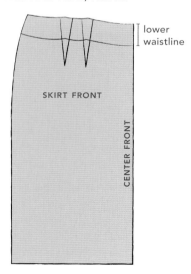

DRAFT A WAISTBAND

Waistbands enclose all the raw edges for a nice neat finish on the top edge of skirts and pants. If the skirt opens with a zipper, the waistband is typically held closed with snaps or hooks, and features an extension, or underlap, on the right side of the skirt opening that goes under the left side of the waistband. There are several ways to draft a waistband, as described below and on the next two pages. Choose the one that works best for you.

One-Piece Waistband with Separate Facing

A traditional waistband is one rectangular piece between 1" and 2" wide. This type of waistband is used when there is a zipper opening at the center front, center back, or left side seam. The illustration shows a skirt with a back zipper placement.

1. To start, measure the top edges of the skirt front and back patterns, minus any darts, seam allowances, or facings. You can start with a one- or two-dart sloper.

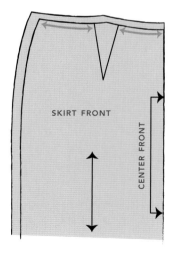

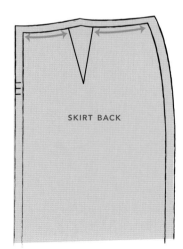

Two-Piece Waistband with Separate Facings

2. Double the measurements for any pieces that are cut twice or on the fold, and add them all together. Since this waistband is used with a zipper, the waistband will need an extra 1" to 1½" extension for the overlap. The illustration shows an extension for a front left side seam.

3. Draw a rectangle equal in dimension to the desired length and width measurements. Add ½" seam allowance around all the edges. (See pages 68–69 for How to Assemble and Attach Your Waistband.) You will cut two waistbands, one to use as the waistband front and the second to use as the waistband facing.

A two-piece waistband is similar to the one-piece waistband; however, the front and back are separate pieces. The two pieces are joined at the sides, creating side seams. Typically this waistband is drafted when the skirt front and back are very different, such as for the wrap skirts in chapter 4, but it can also be used for a skirt with a side zipper. Again, cut two waistbands, one for the waistband front and one for the waistband facing.

1. To start, measure the top edges of the skirt front and back patterns separately, minus any darts, seam allowances, or facings.

2. Treat the front and back separately. Double the measurements for any pieces that are cut twice or on the fold, and add the front measurements together and the back measurements together. If the skirt has a side zipper, add an extra 1" to 1½" extension to the front waistband for the overlap.

3. For the front and the back, draw a rectangle equal in dimension to the desired length and width measurements. Add ½" seam allowance around all the edges, including the side seams, but excluding any edges to be cut on the fold. (See pages 68–69 for How to Assemble and Attach Your Waistband.)

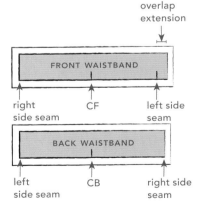

overlap extension

FRONT WAISTBAND

right side seam   CF   left side seam

BACK WAISTBAND

left side seam   CB   right side seam

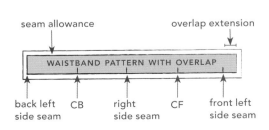

seam allowance   overlap extension

WAISTBAND PATTERN WITH OVERLAP

back left side seam   CB   right side seam   CF   front left side seam

Two-Piece Contoured Waistband with Separate Facings

A contoured waistband is specially shaped to fit the curves of the body, so it lies against the waistline without any gaps. When the skirt opens at the side seam, the front waistband is cut as one piece and the back waistband is cut as another.

1. Trace the slopers onto pattern drafting paper to make the waistband pattern. You can start with a one- or two-dart sloper. Lower the waistline (page 65) if desired or keep it at the natural waist. Then draw the waistband seamline parallel to the top edge and the desired width from the top edge on both the skirt front and back. Cut off the waistband from both patterns and save them.

2. Fold the darts closed on both the front and back waistband patterns and blend away any sharp edges. Since you'll be using the bottom of the sloper for the skirt body patterns, blend those top edges as well. If the skirt has a zipper or button opening that ends below the waistband, the waistband will need an extension or underlap; in that case, add an extra 1" to 1½" for the extension. Add ½" seam allowances all around the pieces. Voila! You've created a custom-fitted waistband! (See the next page for How to Assemble and Attach Your Waistband.)

note

If the skirt opens in the center front, the front waistband is cut as two pieces to allow for the garment opening; the same applies if the skirt opens in the center back. The waistband would then be three pieces.

drop waistline

waistband seamline

SKIRT FRONT

CENTER FRONT

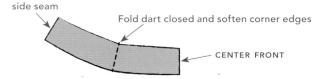

side seam

Fold dart closed and soften corner edges

CENTER FRONT

HOW TO ASSEMBLE AND ATTACH YOUR WAISTBAND

ONE-PIECE WAISTBAND AND SEPARATE FACING

1. After drafting the waistband and adding seam allowance, cut two pieces from fabric. One waistband will become the waistband facing. Cut one waistband from interfacing. Fuse the interfacing to the wrong side of one waistband piece, following the manufacturer's instructions.

2. Assemble the skirt and then attach the waistband as follows. Pin the interfaced waistband to the skirt with the right sides together and raw edges aligned.

   a) *If you do not have an extension* (for instance the edge of a wrap skirt), position the waistband ends so they extend ½" past the skirt opening edges.

   b) *If you do have an extension,* position the waistband end to extend beyond the skirt opening (on the left side only) by the drafted length of the extension plus seam allowance.

3. Stitch the waistband to the top of the skirt. Press the seam allowances toward the waistband.

4. Pin the waistband facing to the top of the waistband with the right sides together and raw edges aligned; stitch. Press the seam allowance toward the facing and understitch (see page 37) ⅛" from the seamline. (Illustration shows waistband without an extension.)

5. Press under the remaining long edge of the facing ½" to the wrong side. Turn the waistband right sides together again.

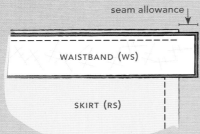

step 2a no extension

seam allowance

WAISTBAND (WS)

SKIRT (RS)

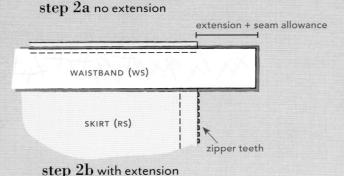

step 2b with extension

extension + seam allowance

WAISTBAND (WS)

SKIRT (RS)

zipper teeth

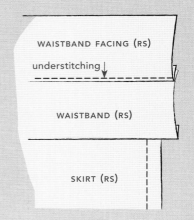

step 4

WAISTBAND (RS)

WAISTBAND FACING (WS)

WAISTBAND SEAMLINE

SKIRT (RS)

WAISTBAND FACING (RS)

understitching

WAISTBAND (RS)

SKIRT (RS)

a) *If there is no waistband extension,* stitch the waistband side seam even with the edge of the skirt.

b) *If the waistband has an extension,* unfold the bottom seam allowances for both waistband and facing. Stitch the side seam, pivot at the bottom edge seam allowance, and stitch along the creased fold to the edge of the skirt. Backstitch.

Trim the corners, turn the waistband right side out, and press.

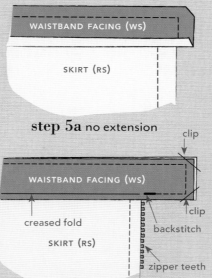

step 5a no extension

step 5b with extension

6. Secure the bottom of the facing to cover the seam allowance with either hand stitches or by stitching in the ditch from the garment's right side.

• *If the waistband has an extension,* hand-sew a hook and eye to finish the waistband. Sew the eye to the extension (or underlap) and the hook to the wrong side of the left edge of the waistband.

TWO-PIECE (STRAIGHT AND CONTOURED) WAISTBAND WITH SEPARATE FACINGS

1. After drafting the waistbands and adding seam allowance, cut two front waistbands and two back waistbands from fabric unless there is an opening in the center back or front, in which case cut two right back (or front) waistbands and two left back (or front) waistbands from fabric. One set of waistbands will become the waistband facing. Cut one of each waistband from interfacing and fuse the interfacing to the wrong side of one set of waistbands, following the manufacturer's instructions.

2. Pin the side seams of the front interfaced waistband to the back interfaced waistband(s), keeping the zipper placement in mind, with the right sides together and raw edges aligned. For a side seam zipper, don't sew the left side seam. For a centered zipper, don't sew the center-back (or front) seam. Repeat with the waistband facing pieces.

3. Repeat steps 2 through 6 for One-Piece Waistband to finish. Make sure the waistband side seams are aligned with the skirt side seams.

TIP You can also stitch in the ditch to close the waistband. To do this, make sure the bottom edge of the waistband on the inside of the skirt extends past the seamline by ⅛". Pin the layers in place, and from the right side machine-stitch directly over the seamline, catching the bottom edge of the waistband inside the skirt. It's called "stitching in the ditch" because your stitch line is sewn inside the indention of the original seamline, hiding the stitches.

DRAFT A WAISTLINE FACING

Unlike a waistband that is visible at the top edge of the skirt, a facing still finishes the top edge, but folds to the wrong side of the skirt. The facing is drafted separately from the skirt on pattern-making paper.

To draft the facing, pin any remaining darts closed. Then, trace the top edge of the skirt front for the front facing and the top edge of the skirt back for the back facing. Continue tracing the lines of the slopers, about 2" to 3" down the side seam and center front or center back onto patternmaking paper. Measure down the same amount from the top edges and draw parallel lines. Trace the drafted facings (do not cut them off). Add ½" seam allowances to all seamed edges.

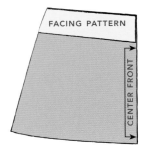

FACING PATTERN

CENTER FRONT

LENGTHEN OR SHORTEN YOUR PATTERN

Your skirt sloper is drafted to span from your true waist to the top of your knee. If you want to change where the bottom edge of your skirt hits your legs, it is easy to lengthen or shorten your design.

Draft a line parallel to the original hemline, somewhere in the center of the sloper, dividing the pattern in half.

- To lengthen the pattern, cut along the newly drafted line and spread the pattern apart the desired amount. Then draw in new side seam, center-front, and center-back lines.

- To shorten the pattern, cut along the newly drafted line and overlap the pattern pieces to achieve the desired length. Then draw in new side seam, center-front, and center-back lines.

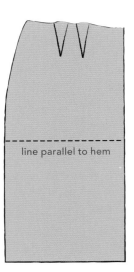

line parallel to hem

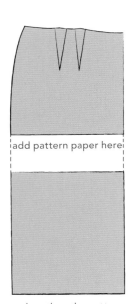

add pattern paper here

to lengthen the pattern

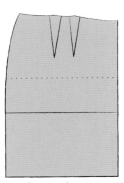

overlap

to shorten the pattern

Finishing Up

What to add before you start sewing

Once you have traced your sloper onto drafting paper and made all the design changes, including drafting a waistband and any other pattern pieces, there are a few elements that should be marked on the paper patterns before you use them to cut out your fabric, including grainline arrows (page 25), registration marks, and any special labels, such as the name of the piece and how many pieces to cut.

SEAM AND HEM ALLOWANCES

Seam and hem allowances are left off a pattern until it is a completed designed and ready to go. Once you are finished drafting your pattern, each seamline requires seam allowance.

Commercial patterns typically use ⅝"-wide seam allowances. However, the garment industry tends to uses ½"-wide seam allowances, which reduces bulk inside your garment. The ½"-wide seam allowances also conserve fabric by allowing more pieces to fit across your material, and they are easier to draft with a ruler.

For the skirts in this book, add ½"-wide seam allowance to all seams. However, you might find it easier to install a zipper with slightly wider seam allowances,

so consider adding ⅝"-wide seam allowances to any seams that will hold a zipper (this is optional). And, for concealed seams like those inside a waistband, ¼"-wide seam allowances are adequate.

Remember to add seam allowance to all the pattern edges that will be joined to another edge; do not add seam allowances to edges that will be placed on the fabric fold. If there is a center-front or center-back seam, remember to add seam allowance. The grainline arrows will indicate if the fabric is to be cut on the fabric fold.

To add seam allowance, align your ruler with your drafted seamline. Then draw the seam allowance parallel to the seamline.

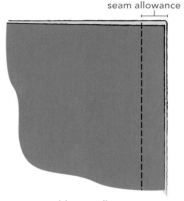

seam allowance

to add seam allowance

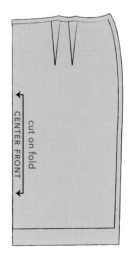

cut on fold
CENTER FRONT

TIP Always write the width of the seam allowance you added somewhere on the pattern or indicate it with a notcher as indicated on the next page.

MARKING

Once you have drafted your own patterns, it's important to mark them correctly so you can remember exactly what you did when you start to sew. A notcher (page 20) is a tool I use frequently in the sewing room to mark things such as seam allowances and dart legs. The following things should be marked on every pattern piece.

Pattern Name. It is so important to label each pattern piece with the name of the design. There have been many times when I was cleaning my sewing room that I accidentally threw out an important element for a pattern, thinking it was rubbish. Clearly label each pattern piece before cutting it out to avoid an untimely demise in the trash can.

Registration Marks. Commercial patterns, such as those from Simplicity, Butterick, and Vogue, draw triangle marks (notches) on the pattern edges to help with registration so you know where to match pieces to sew them together. You can add similar marks to your patterns to remind you how the pieces should be assembled once they are cut apart. A notcher is the perfect tool for making registration marks.

Be sure to make registration marks on all seamlines, including the center front and center back. Typically the center front is marked with two registration marks, while the center back is indicated with three marks. For instance, in the Block Party Skirt (see page 138), registration marks were added to each seamline as a reminder of which pieces needed to be sewn together.

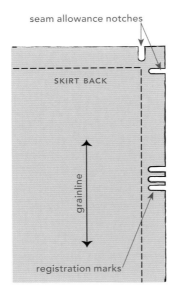

seam allowance notches

SKIRT BACK

grainline

registration marks

Seam allowances. As a reminder of how much seam allowance you added to a pattern, you can mark the width of a seam allowance by notching the pattern at one end of the seam. You can also use this method to mark hem allowances.

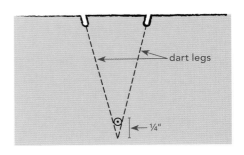

dart legs

¼"

Darts. It's important to mark the top edge and point of the darts. If you have a notcher, use it to mark the dart legs at the top edge of the skirt or simply cut a notch. You can use an awl (page 20) to mark the dart point ¼" inside the point and then circle it with a pencil.

Design Elements. Once all the design elements are clearly drawn on your patterns, it helps to add marks for easier matching and sewing. For items like patch pockets and appliqués, use an awl to poke holes in the pattern ¼" inside the cutting lines. Circle the holes so that you can see them clearly later.

For the Pocket Change Skirt on page 85, I added two military-style pockets on the skirt fronts. To remember where I should place the pockets later, I added placement dots with an awl.

Using Your Sloper

How to make the skirts in this book

The projects in this book are based on four basic skirt silhouettes. They include a wrap, straight, flared, and high-waisted skirt. With a few alterations to your custom sloper, you can create personalized fit and many design variations for any of these four styles. Each skirt will be tailor-made for your body. The following chapters will explain how to draft new patterns for each of the four silhouettes. You will then be able to use the four new versions to make the skirts in the chapters.

It's a good idea to make a muslin or test version of each of the four silhouettes, using the specific pattern that you create from your custom sloper (wrap skirt on page 74, straight skirt on page 116, flared skirt on page 161, and high-waisted skirt on page 196). This way you will be sure of the outcome before you cut any fashion fabric. You don't have to make the waistband or insert a zipper to check for fit; simply make the front and back pieces and stitch them together. Make any necessary alterations on the test skirt and transfer the alterations to the pattern, then you'll be all set to make perfect-fitting skirts for every day of the week.

wrap   straight   flared   high waisted

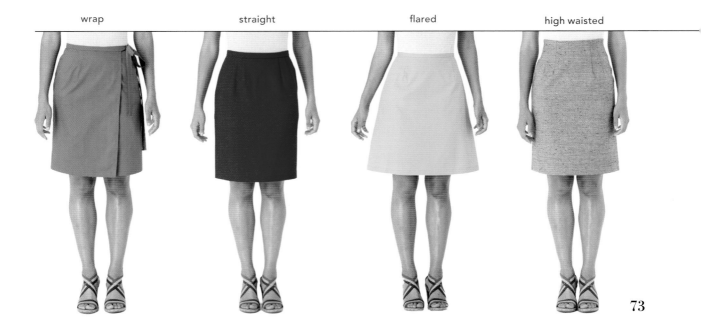

chapter 4
WRAP SKIRTS

Wrap skirts are ideal first projects for designers of all skill levels. They are the simplest skirt variations to draft and sew, plus they are easy to alter and super fun to embellish. There are no fussy closures like zippers or buttons to worry about, and the fit is forgiving, making the pattern drafting a little less stressful. Although this silhouette sometimes seems a bit retro, it can be updated and made quite chic with modern fabrics and a few stylish design details.

A wrap skirt features an overlap of skirt layers to help it stay closed. That overlap can be located on any part of the skirt and can be held closed with ties, snaps, buttons, or even buckles, depending on your design. For modesty's sake, the extensions, or underlap and overlap, are typically at least 3" wide, providing 6" of overlap. Feel free to make the overlapped sections wider if you prefer.

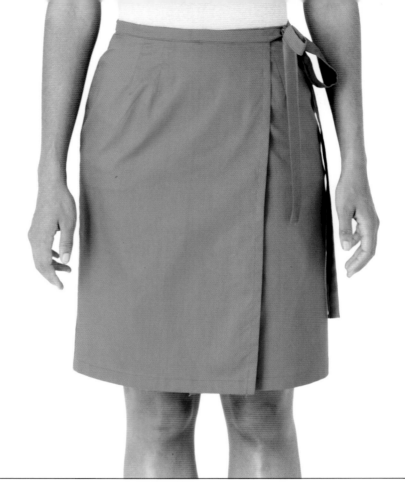

Wrap Skirt

Draft the Basic Pattern

To draft a basic wrap skirt pattern, start with your customized sloper (see chapter 3) and take it from there, as instructed on these pages. The back of the skirt remains the same; to create the wrap, two front pattern pieces are extended so they overlap one another. For most of the wrap skirt projects, the overlap is located at the center front or off to one side.

Draft the Pattern

1. **To draft the skirt front,** trace your customized skirt front sloper onto drafting paper. Draw a new center front approximately 3" over from and parallel to the original center front, as shown. Extend the top and bottom edges to meet the new design line.

2. **To draft the skirt back,** trace your skirt back sloper on paper and indicate that the center back should be positioned on the fabric fold, with a grainline arrow as shown.

3. **To draft the waistband,** see pages 65–67. There are several ways to draft either a one-piece or two-piece waistband or a contoured waistband. The one drafted for this skirt is a two-piece waistband and is ¾" wide. The ties are not drafted on paper, but measured and cut directly on the fabric.

4. **Complete the pattern.** Do not add seam and hem allowances until you are finished with all design work. If you want to make this skirt as is, add seam allowances to any edge that will be joined to another. Typically, ½"-wide seam allowances are most suitable (page 30). Add a 1" hem allowance to the center-front edge, for a ½" double-fold hem. Add hem allowance as desired to the bottom of the skirt.

PATTERN DRAFTING NOTE

Once you draft your basic wrap skirt patterns, before adding seam and hem allowances, copy them onto patternmaking or drafting paper so you can use them as the starting point for several of the wrap skirts in this chapter.

For closing options, such as the ties shown here, or for buttons and snaps, refer to the specific project instructions. To duplicate the ties shown, see page 80.

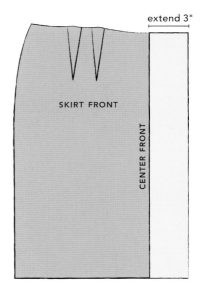

step 1

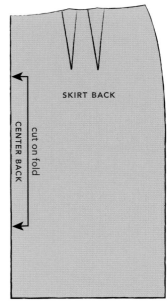

step 2

Sew the Wrap Skirt

SUPPLIES

> 1½ yards of 44/45" fabric

> ½ yard of fusible interfacing

> Matching thread

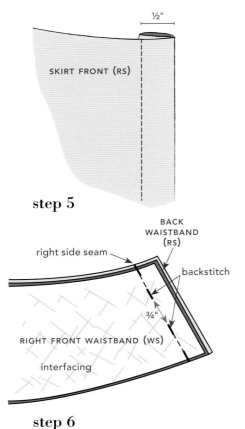

step 5

step 6

BACK
WAISTBAND
(RS)

right side seam

backstitch

¾"

RIGHT FRONT WAISTBAND (WS)

interfacing

½"

SKIRT FRONT (RS)

1. **Cut out the fabric.** Use the newly drafted pattern pieces to cut the following:

   - *From fabric:* two skirt fronts and four front waistbands; and on the fabric fold, one skirt back and two back waistbands.

   - *From interfacing:* two front waistbands, and one back waistband on the fold.

   Cut two ties the desired length × 2" wide, plus seam allowance. The finished ties for this skirt are 29" and 44¼" long. They are different lengths because one wraps farther around the body. (See the tip on the opposite page.)

2. **Apply the interfacing.** Following the manufacturer's instructions, fuse the interfacing to the wrong side of two front and one back waistband.

3. **Stitch the darts in each piece.** Press the darts flat and then toward the center front or center back of the skirt pieces.

4. **Sew the side seams.** With the right sides together, machine-stitch each skirt front to the skirt back along the side seams. Press the seam allowances open and clean finish as desired (pages 33–35).

5. **Finish the skirt front and bottom edges.** Press a ½" double-fold hem on the two front raw edges and the bottom edge, topstitching the front edges in place. Topstitch or hand-sew the hem as desired.

6. **Assemble the waistband.** With the right sides together and raw edges aligned, stitch the interfaced front waistbands to the interfaced back waistband along the side seams. Leave a ¾" break in the stitching in the right side seam (this is for the tie end to slip through). Be sure to backstitch at the beginning and end of the

break in the stitching. Press the seam allowances open. Repeat to assemble the waistband facing (non-interfaced waistband pieces).

7. **Make and attach the ties.** Press under the long edges and one narrow edge of each tie ¼" to the wrong side. Press the ties in half with the wrong sides together (raw edges tucked inside) and edge-stitch them closed.

   Baste the narrow (unfinished) end of the shorter tie to the right front skirt, in the center and on the right side of the interfaced waistband with the raw edges aligned.

   In the same way, baste the narrow (unfinished) end of the longer tie to the left front, in the center and on the right side of the inter-faced waistband with the raw edges aligned.

8. **Attach the waistband.** With the right sides together and raw edges aligned, pin the interfaced waistband to the skirt, with the side seams aligned. Each waistband end should extend past the skirt front edge by ½". Include the basted tie ends in the seam. Stitch and press the seam allowances toward the waistband.

9. **To face and finish the waistband,** refer to How to Assemble and Attach Your Waistband on pages 68–69, steps 4–6.

10. **Hand-slipstitch** (page 29) the waistband and facing together at the opening in the side seam so the slit remains open but the edges are clean finished.

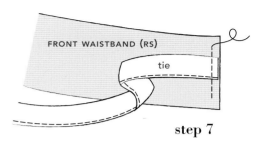

step 7

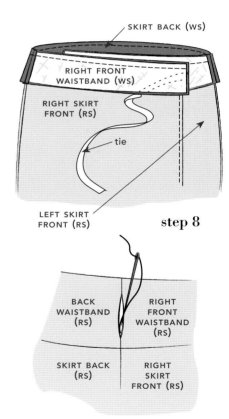

step 8

step 10

TIP Tie a sash or even a tape measure around your waist to determine a good length for the ties, or cut them extra long so you can adjust them to the desired length once the skirt is finished.

SUNDAY

Spot On Wrap Skirt

Design Variation: Patch Pockets and Contoured Waistband

If you don't like wearing garments that come all the way up to your true waist, don't worry, lowering a waistline is an easy alteration that can be completed in a snap (see page 65). Once you drop the waistline, you can add a wide, contoured waistband and a patch pocket. If you've ever tried on garments and found a gap between the small of the back and the garment's waistband, try this contoured technique for a waistband that is custom-cut to fit your body and follow your curves.

Draft the Pattern

1. **Trace your basic wrap skirt slopers** onto drafting paper. Make sure the pattern doesn't have any seam or hem allowances included yet. Complete steps 1 and 2 for the basic wrap skirt pattern (see page 77).

2. **Lower the waistline** of the skirt front and back by 1½" (see page 65).

3. **Draft the waistband.** Determine how wide you want the waistband to be and measure down from the (lowered) top edge of both the skirt front and skirt back by this amount. (The waistband on this skirt is 2" wide.) Cut off the waistband, but save it for help drafting the contoured waistband in step 5.

4. **Adjust darts as needed.** If the new waistband design line was not dropped below the dart points, measure any remaining dart width. Remove the measured amount from the side seam, and blend the new side seamline. Do this for both the skirt front and back.

5. **Draft a two-piece contoured waistband** using the waistband sections you cut off in step 3. Follow the directions on page 67 to close the darts and finish the pattern. For the front waistband pieces, the waistband should extend to the edge of the extension. Repeat to draft the back waistband, and mark it so the center back is cut on the fabric fold. Ties will not be drafted on paper, but measured and cut from bias tape.

PATTERN DRAFTING NOTE
You can lower the waistline for a more natural fit on almost any skirt design. The waistline on the skirt shown here was lowered 1½", but you can lower it as much or as little as you wish.

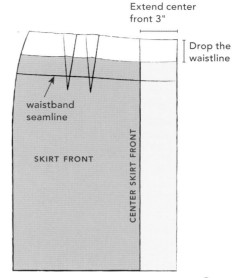

Extend center front 3"

Drop the waistline

waistband seamline

SKIRT FRONT

CENTER SKIRT FRONT

step 3

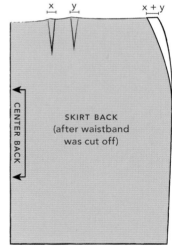

x y   x + y

CENTER BACK

SKIRT BACK (after waistband was cut off)

step 4

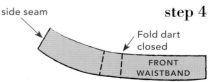

side seam

Fold dart closed

FRONT WAISTBAND

step 5

> 1½ yards of 44/45" fabric

> 1 yard of fusible interfacing

> 3 yards of double-fold
  bias tape

> Matching thread

6. **Add the seam and hem allowances.** Add 1" hem allowance to the skirt front edges, 2" for the bottom edge, and ½" seam allowances for all other seams. For more help on hem and seam allowances, see pages 45–51.

7. **Draw a pocket pattern as desired.** You can leave the bottom edges as right angles or round them into curves. You can even make the top edge asymmetrical; it's all up to you! It might help to measure the size of a favorite pocket on a skirt or pair of pants that you own. Once you are satisfied with the size and shape of the pocket, add ¼" hem allowance to the sides and bottom edge, and add 1" to the top edge.

Sew the Spot On Skirt

1. **Cut out the fabric.** Use the newly drafted pattern pieces to cut the following:

   • *From fabric:* two skirt fronts and one skirt back on the fabric fold, four front waistbands and two back waistbands on the fabric fold, and one pocket.

   • *From interfacing:* two front waistbands and one back waistband on the fold.

2. **Apply interfacing.** Following the manufacturer's instructions, fuse the interfacing to the wrong side of two front waistbands and one back waistband.

DESIGN NOTE
I used double-fold bias tape cut from contrasting fabric for the ties and as a detail on the pocket. However, you can use premade bias tape, or even ribbon instead.

3. **Sew the side seams.** With the right sides together, machine-stitch each skirt front to the skirt back along the side seams. Press the seam allowances open.

4. **Finish the skirt front and bottom edges.** Press a ½" double-fold hem on the two front raw edges. Repeat for the bottom edge, turning under 1" twice. Topstitch the front edges in place. Topstitch or hand-sew the hem as desired.

5. **Make the ties from bias tape** by cutting a length of bias tape for each tie. Cut them both long enough to wrap around your waist. You can always cut them shorter once the skirt is made (the ties for this skirt are 24" and 27" long). Edgestitch the open edge of the bias tape closed. Save a long enough piece of bias tape to finish the top edge of the pocket.

6. **Assemble and attach the waistband** as for the basic wrap skirt (page 79), except substitute the bias tape ties for the fabric ties.

7. **Make and attach the patch pocket.** Cut a 1-inch strip of interfacing as wide as your pocket and fuse it to the top edge on the fabric's wrong side.

   To help with pressing under the edges, trace your pocket pattern onto Kraft paper and then cut off all hem allowances. Center the paper pocket on the fabric pocket's wrong side and use it as a guide for pressing under the ¼" seam allowance on the sides and bottom and 1" along the top interfacing edge.

   Topstitch the top edge in place close to the raw edge (about ⅞" from the folded top edge). If you want to embellish the top edge with bias tape, add that now.

   Place the pocket on your skirt and check that the top edge is parallel with the top of the skirt. Topstitch in place along the bottom and side edges.

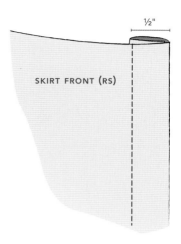

step 4

step 7

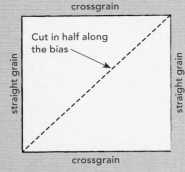

crossgrain

Cut in half along the bias

straight grain

straight grain

crossgrain

step 1

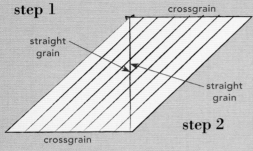

crossgrain

straight grain

straight grain

crossgrain

step 2

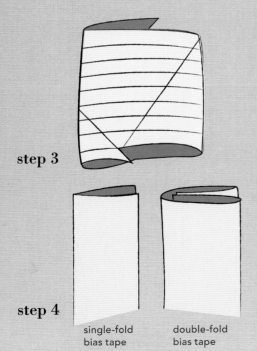

step 3

step 4

single-fold bias tape

double-fold bias tape

MAKE YOUR OWN BIAS TAPE

You can purchase ready-made bias tape in a variety of colors and widths, or you can make your own from any fabric you like. It's great to use bias tape to finish raw edges, whether it's on a hemline or as a Hong Kong seam finish (page 33). The following steps explain a favorite method for creating a continuous strip of bias tape that you can use on almost any type of fabric. Decide how wide you want the finished bias tape and then cut strips as below.

- *For single-fold bias tape,* mark and cut the fabric strips 2 times the desired finished width.
- *For double-fold bias tape,* mark and cut the fabric strips 4 times the desired finished width.

1. **Cut your fabric into a perfect square,** and label the crossgrain and straight grain sides using a temporary fabric marker (page 15). Draw a diagonal line bisecting the square and cut along the marked (bias) line.

2. **Stitch the two halves** with the right sides and straight grain edges together. Draw lines parallel to the bias edge the predetermined width apart (see bullets above) with a temporary fabric marker, as shown.

3. **Stitch the two crossgrain edges** with the right sides together and raw edges aligned; however, offset the edges by one strip width as shown. To finish, cut the strips along the marked lines.

4. **To create single-fold bias tape,** simply fold the tape in half with long edges aligned and wrong sides together, and press.

   For double-fold bias tape, fold the tape in half as you would a single-fold tape and press. Then fold the two raw edges in toward the center and press again.

Pocket Change Skirt

Design Variation:
Center-Front Opening and
Military Bellows Pockets

Drafting bellows pockets may look tricky, but they really only require a few straight lines. You can draft bellows pockets of any size — perfect for pants, skirts, and even handbags. I used buttons as a closure on the pockets shown here, but you can simplify the process by using snaps or even Velcro, or having no closure at all.

MONDAY

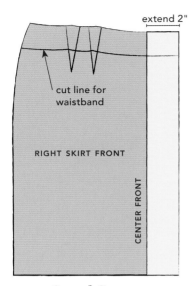

extend 2"

cut line for
waistband

RIGHT SKIRT FRONT

CENTER FRONT

steps 2 and 3

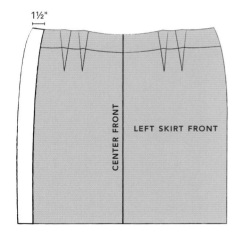

1½"

CENTER FRONT

LEFT SKIRT FRONT

step 4

Draft the Pattern

1. **Trace your customized basic front and back skirt slopers** onto drafting paper. Make sure the pattern doesn't have any seam or hem allowances included yet. You'll need to draft separate right (upper-layer) and left (under-layer) front skirt pieces.

2. **Draft the right front** by extending the center front as far as you would like. The center front of the skirt shown was extended 2" to create a facing along the front edge.

3. **Design the waistband.** Determine how wide you want the waistband. Measure down and mark a line parallel to the top edge of the skirt this amount.

4. **Draft the left front.** With a center front opening, extend the underneath layer (left front) nearly to the opposite side seam for modesty coverage. To draft this piece, trace the *original* skirt front (without the extension), then flip it over and trace it again with the center fronts aligned. Trim off 1½" from the right side seam. This will all be cut as one piece. Repeat step 3 to mark the waistband.

5. **Draft the front waistbands** Cut off the right front and left front waistbands. Close the darts and smooth the edges to create contoured right and left front waistbands (see page 67). Add ½" seam allowance all the way around and make sure to label each.

6. **Draft the skirt back.** Label the center back to be cut on the fold. Measure down from the top edge the same amount as in step 3. Cut off the waistband and close the darts as in step 5. Indicate that the waistband should be cut on the fold just like the skirt back. Add ½" seam allowance to all but the center-back edge.

7. **Add ½" seam allowances** and 2" hem allowances to the skirt front and back patterns.

8. **Draft the pocket.** First, draw a rectangle as wide and long as you want your finished pocket to be. If you're not sure, measure the pocket on a favorite garment. Add 1" to the top and ¾" to both side and bottom edges. Do not add anything to the bottom corners, as shown. Then, add ¼" seam allowance to all the pocket edges, including the corners.

9. **Draft the pocket flap.** Draw the pocket flap pattern shaped as shown, with the center approximately ⅓ the finished height of your pocket from step 8. Draw the flap width equal to the width of the finished pocket plus ¼". Add ¼" seam allowances to all the edges.

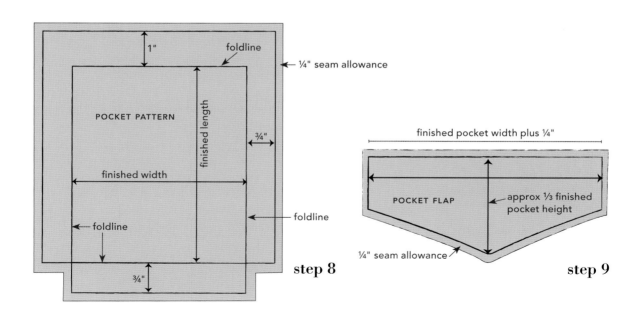

step 8

step 9

Sew the Pocket Change Skirt

SUPPLIES

> 2⅓ yards of 44/45" fabric

> ¾ yard of fusible interfacing

> 3 buttons

> Matching thread

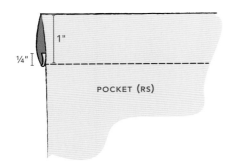

step 3a

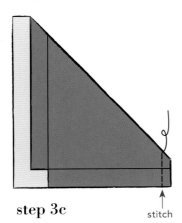

step 3c

stitch

1. **Cut out the fabric.** Use the newly drafted pattern pieces to cut the following:

    *   *From fabric:* one right and one left skirt front, two right front waist-bands, two left front waistbands, two pockets and four pocket flaps. On the fabric fold, cut one back skirt and two back waistbands.

    *   *From interfacing:* one right front waistband, one left front waist-band, two pocket flaps, and one back waistband on the fold. Transfer the marked foldlines on the pattern to the fabric with a temporary fabric marker.

2. **Apply interfacing.** Following the manufacturer's instructions, fuse the interfacing to the wrong side of corresponding fabric pieces as listed in step 1.

3. **Sew the pockets,** as follows:

    a) Cut two strips of interfacing 1" × the width of the top edge of the pocket. Fuse the interfacing on the wrong side of each pocket, ¼" below the top edge. Press under the top edge of the pockets ¼" and then 1" to the wrong side. Topstitch close to the inside folded edge of both pockets (see step 7 illustration).

    b) Press under the side and bottom edges 1" to the wrong side along the marked foldlines.

    c) With the right sides together, fold one bottom edge to the closest side edge, as shown. The marked foldlines should align. Stitch the corner with ¼" seam allowance. Repeat for the other side. Turn the pocket right side out and press the seam allowances along the bottom and sides ¼" to the wrong side.

CONSTRUCTION NOTE

Take your time assembling the bellows pockets. They aren't difficult to sew, but can be a little tricky at the corners. You can omit the pocket flap if you prefer, depending on your design.

4. **Assemble the flaps** using ¼" seam allowance. With the right sides together and raw edges aligned, stitch one interfaced flap to one non-interfaced flap along the side and bottom edges. Trim the corners and turn the flaps right side out. Press, and then baste the top edges together. Topstitch around the sides and bottom edges. Press the top edges to one side along the basting stitches. If you are planning on buttons, stitch buttonholes in the flaps now, making sure the length fits your buttons (see page 38).

5. **Stitch any remaining darts** in the skirt fronts and back. Press them toward the center of the skirt.

6. **Sew the side seams.** With the right sides together and raw edges aligned, stitch each skirt front to the skirt back along the side seams. Press the seam allowances open, and clean finish as desired (pages 33–35).

7. **Attach the pockets. a)** Position the pockets wherever you want them on the skirt, and pin them in place along the pressed edges. Edgestitch each pocket in place along the bottom fold of the side and bottom edges.

   b) For extra security, you can secure and stitch down the top edges of each corner, through all the layers as shown.

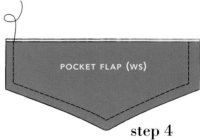

POCKET FLAP (WS)

step 4

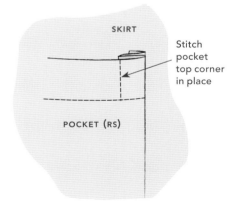

SKIRT

Stitch pocket top corner in place

POCKET (RS)

step 7b

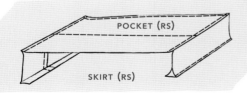

POCKET (RS)

SKIRT (RS)

step 7a

DESIGN NOTE

For added dimension, you can edgestitch along the side and bottom foldlines with the wrong sides of the pocket together.

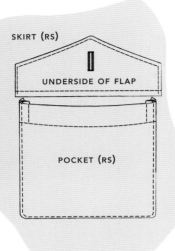

SKIRT (RS)

UNDERSIDE OF FLAP

POCKET (RS)

step 8

8. **Attach the flaps.** Center each flap ⅛" above each pocket as shown. Stitch the flaps in place ¼" from the edge. Then, press each flap down over the top of the pockets and edgestitch ¼" from the fold. This will cover the bottom raw edge of the pocket.

9. **Finish the left skirt front edge** by pressing under a 1" double-fold hem. Topstitch close to the inner pressed edge. The right skirt front edge has a fold-back facing, so press under the raw edge ½" to the wrong side and then another 2". Topstitch close to the inside folded edge to create the facing as shown in the photograph.

10. **Assemble and attach the two-piece contoured waistband** with separate facing as explained on page 69.

11. **Finish the skirt.** Stitch a horizontal buttonhole on the right front waistband (page 38). Then try on the skirt and mark the snap location to secure the left front edge. Take off the skirt and hand-sew a snap and the three buttons in place (pages 38–39). Carefully press under the lower edge of the skirt ½" to the wrong side and then another 1½". Topstitch close to the inner folded edge, or sew the hem as desired (pages 45–51).

TUESDAY

Spring-Loaded Wrap Skirt

Design Variations:
Ruched Waistband, In-Seam Pockets,
and Optional Appliqué

I love in-seam pockets. They're invisible from the outside, but they're always there when you need them to help keep important items close at hand. This waistband features a feminine gathered panel that's easy to stitch and still packs a stylish punch. And the appliqué is a simple way to add personality to any skirt, or even breathe new life into an old favorite in your closet.

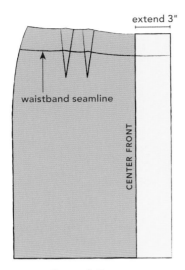

extend 3"

waistband seamline

CENTER FRONT

steps 1 and 2

Draft the Pattern

1. **Trace your basic wrap skirt slopers** onto drafting paper. Make sure the patterns don't have any seam or hem allowances included yet. Complete steps 1 and 2 as for the basic wrap skirt (page 77), which includes adding a 3" extension (add a wider extension if desired).

2. **Lower the waistline** (page 65), if desired. Then, draw the waistband seamline the desired distance from the top edge on both front and the back skirt patterns. (The waistband shown is about 2½" wide.)

3. **Make the waistband.** Cut off the waistband along the newly marked lines and follow the directions for a contour waistband on page 67, but do not add seam allowances yet. Use a curved ruler to smooth out the bend where the darts have been closed.

PATTERN DRAFTING NOTE

This dress has a complete waistband (front and facing) made out of the main fabric. A ruched waistband, made from the contrasting fabric, is drafted wider than the original waistband, gathered top to bottom, and stitched on top of the front waistband.

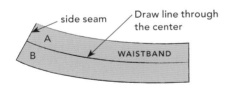

side seam / Draw line through the center

A
B
WAISTBAND

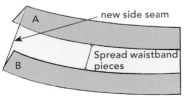

A
B
new side seam
Spread waistband pieces

step 4

4. **Draft the ruched waistband.** Trace the front and back waistband pieces onto pattern-drafting paper. Working on one waistband at a time, draw a line through the center as shown and cut the pattern in half along the line. Spread the two pieces apart at the cut line, until the new width is about 1½ times the original width (for a 2½" waistband, add 1½"). Tape the spread pieces to paper. Neaten the side edges by drawing a new line from the original bottom edge to the original top edge. Repeat for the remaining pieces and label them.

5. **Draw the in-seam pocket.** Trace a copy of the skirt front, especially the top and side seam edges. Draw your desired pocket on the traced skirt, making sure it's as deep and as wide as you would like. Then, trace the pocket only, following the top edge of the skirt for the top edge of the pocket, and the side seam of the skirt for the side edge of the pocket.

6. **Draft two ties** as wide as the *ruched* waistband patterns and 36" long.

7. **Complete the pattern.** Add ½" seam allowances around all the patterns and a 2" hem allowance to the bottom edges (or as wide as desired, depending on the fabric weight, pages 45–51). Just remember that any raw edge that will be joined to another needs seam allowance.

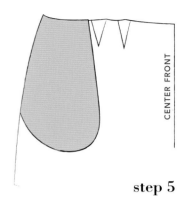

CENTER FRONT

step 5

TIP If you want to be sure the pocket will accommodate your hand, simply place your hand on the paper, and draw around it.

Sew the Spring-Loaded Wrap Skirt

1. **Cut out the fabric.** Use the newly drafted pattern pieces to cut the following:

   - *From main skirt fabric:* two skirt fronts and one skirt back on the fabric fold, four front waistbands and two back waistbands on the fabric fold, and four pockets.

   - *From contrasting fabric:* two ruched front waistbands, one ruched back waistband on the fabric fold, two ties, and appliqués as desired (see How to Appliqué, page 97).

   - *From interfacing:* two front waistbands and one back waistband on the fold.

SUPPLIES

> **2 yards of 44/45" fabric**

> **1⅓ yards of contrasting 44/45" print fabric**

> **¾ yard of fusible interfacing**

> **Double-sided fusible web (for optional appliqué)**

> **1 snap**

> **Matching thread**

2. **Apply interfacing.** Following the manufacturer's instructions, fuse the interfacing to the wrong side of two front waistbands and one back waistband.

3. **Stitch the darts.** If the lower portion of any darts remain after lowering the waistline and cutting off the pattern for the waistband, stitch the darts in the skirt front and back (for help on darts, turn to page 35).

4. **Attach the pockets.** With right sides together and raw edges aligned, pin one pocket to the upper side seam corner on both skirt fronts and to the upper side corners on the back. Stitch the side seam, and then press the pocket and seam allowance out to the side of the skirt.

5. **Sew the side seams.** Both sides of the skirt fronts and skirt backs should now have pocket pieces attached. With the right sides together, side seams aligned, and pockets extended, stitch the two fronts to the skirt back from the bottom edge, up the side seam to just above the pocket, and then pivot to stitch around each pocket. Then, stitch the side seam from the top edge down for about 1". Press the seam allowance open. Then press the pockets toward the skirt front and baste them in place across the top edge.

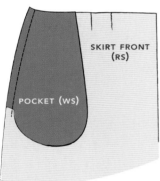

SKIRT FRONT (RS)

POCKET (WS)

step 4

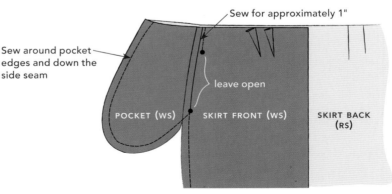

Sew for approximately 1"

Sew around pocket edges and down the side seam

leave open

POCKET (WS)   SKIRT FRONT (WS)   SKIRT BACK (RS)

step 5

6. **Finish the skirt front and bottom edges.** Press under and stitch a 1" double-fold hem to hide the raw edges. Press the hem allowance to the wrong side and hem as desired (pages 45–51).

7. **Gather the waistband. a)** Run one or two rows of basting stitches along each short end of the expanded waistband pieces, backstitching at one end.

   b) Pull the bobbin thread to gather the waistband until it is the same width as the waistband facing. Knot to secure the pulled basting stitches.

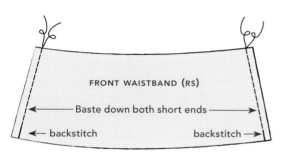

step 7a   step 7b

8. **Make the ties.** Turn under a narrow ¼" hem on one short and both long edges of each tie and stitch.

9. **Pin each gathered waistband** to a corresponding interfaced waistband piece with *wrong* sides together and raw edges aligned. Baste around the edges to secure the layers together. With the right sides together and raw edges aligned, pin and stitch one tie to the right front waistband at the center front edge with the finished edges of the tie ½" from the top and bottom of the waistband. Save the remaining tie for a later step.

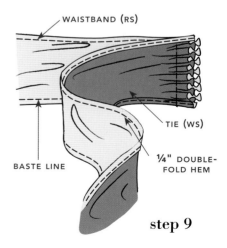

step 9

10. **Assemble the waistband.** Pin the three outer waistband pieces from step 9 at the side seams with right sides together and raw edges aligned and stitch the sides to make one long waistband (with the right front tie end attached). Then pin the waistband to the skirt with right sides together, so the side seams match up, and the raw edges align. The tie end-seam should line up with the hemmed edge of the right front. Stitch, and then press the seam allowance toward the waistband.

11. **Face the waistband.** With the right sides together, stitch the remaining waistband facing pieces together at the side seams to create one long waistband facing. Press under one long edge and both short edges ½" to the wrong side. Pin and stitch the waistband facing to the attached waistband along the top edge with right sides together and edges aligned (see page 68). Press the seam allowances toward the facing and understitch. Fold the waistband to the wrong side so it covers the waistline seam; hand-sew the pressed facing edges to the waistband at the front edges and along the waistline seam. This will encase the tie end/waistband seam.

12. **Attach the remaining tie end.** Press the raw edge of the remaining tie end to the wrong side. Edgestitch the folded edge at the left side seam so the tie end extends toward the front of the skirt.

13. **Finish the skirt.** Try on the skirt, tying the tie ends. Mark the desired location for a snap at the left front edge. Take off the skirt and hand-sew a snap in place.

HOW TO APPLIQUÉ

Appliqué is one of my most favorite embellishment techniques. It's easy to master and breathes new life into any old (or new) clothing. Use a bold print and simple stitching for extra pizzazz. It's also a great technique to use in craft and home décor projects.

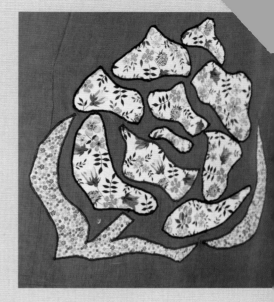

1. Select and cut out the desired motif from your print fabric. Cut so there is about a 1" border around the motif. Then, cut a piece of double-sided fusible web in the same shape.

2. Follow the manufacturer's instructions to fuse the web onto the wrong side of the appliqué. Do not remove the paper backing yet. Trim away the extra border of fabric around the motif to define and shape the actual appliqué.

3. Follow the manufacturer's instructions to fuse the appliqué to the desired location on the garment.

4. Machine zigzag around the edges of the appliqué to secure it to the garment and prevent the edges from fraying. You can use matching or contrasting thread for extra detail.

TIP / When selecting your appliqué fabric, keep the care instructions for your project in mind because you don't want to add a dry-clean-only appliqué to a garment you want to throw into the washing machine.

Double-Time Wrap Skirt

Design Variation:
Reversible Skirt and Scalloped Hem

Double your fun with a reversible skirt that is two garments in one. For even more versatility, make one side from a casual fabric for day, and choose a coordinating elegant fabric for the other side. If you want, you can omit the scalloped edge, making this project even quicker to sew.

WEDNESDAY

Draft the Pattern

1. **Trace your basic customized skirt slopers** (see chapter 3) onto drafting paper. Make sure the pattern doesn't have any seam or hem allowances included yet. Adjust the patterns so they only have one dart in the front and back (page 64).

2. **Make the front extension.** Trace the new skirt front onto drafting/pattern paper. Flip it over and trace it again facedown, with the center fronts aligned to make one whole front skirt.

3. **Trace the skirt back** onto the same pattern paper with the side seam aligned with the right side of the front. Draw a curved line as shown on the left front side, starting at the waist, curving to the hem at the center front.

4. **Draw a scalloped edge** along the left side edge and hem, starting at the center back. You can use a can or large roll of tape as a template.

5. **Add seam allowances.** Add a ½" seam allowance to the top edge and ¼" seam allowance to the dart at the side seam and to the scalloped hem. Be sure to add the hem allowance so it follows the curve of the scalloped edge.

6. **Make a waistband pattern.** Measure across the top edge of the entire skirt, not including the darts or seam allowances. Draw a rectangle equal in length to this measurement plus 4" long (for extension) × ¾" wide. Add ½" seam allowance all around.

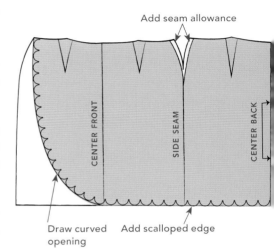

Add seam allowance

CENTER FRONT

SIDE SEAM

CENTER BACK

Draw curved opening

Add scalloped edge

step 3

PATTERN DRAFTING NOTE

This technique eliminates the side seams, transforming them into darts. The skirt shown is a wrap skirt, but you can use this method to eliminate side seams for any skirt, which is helpful if you don't want to cut through a fabric print or border.

Sew the Double-Time Wrap Skirt

SUPPLIES

> 2 yards of 44/45" outside fabric
> 2 yards of 44/45" inside fabric
> 1 yard of fusible interfacing
> 2 hook and eyes
> Matching thread
> Pinking shears (optional)

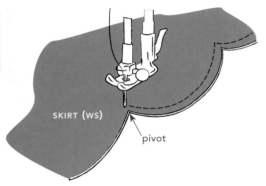

SKIRT (WS)

pivot

1. **Cut out both fabrics.** Use the newly drafted pattern to cut the following pieces. *It is important to cut the skirt faceup on the right side of one fabric and facedown on the right side of the other fabric.*

   - *From the outside fabric:* one skirt with the center back on the fabric fold and two waistbands on the fabric fold.

   - *From the inside fabric:* same pieces as the outside fabric.

   - *From interfacing:* one waistband.

2. **Apply interfacing.** Following the manufacturer's instructions, fuse the interfacing to the wrong side of one waistband.

3. **Stitch the darts.** With the right sides together stitch the darts on both the inside and outside skirts. Stitch the side seam darts with ¼" seam allowance.

4. **Attach the two skirts.** With the right sides together and scalloped edges aligned, stitch the two skirts together along the edges. To stitch a smooth scalloped edge, leave the needle in the fabric at the top point of each scallop, lift the presser foot, and pivot the fabric. Lower the presser foot and continue stitching.

DESIGN NOTE

This skirt is reversible, so you'll need an inside fabric (or lining), and an outside fabric. Choose two fabrics you love so you can show off both sides. Because this skirt is double-sided, choose lighter-weight fabrics that won't get too bulky.

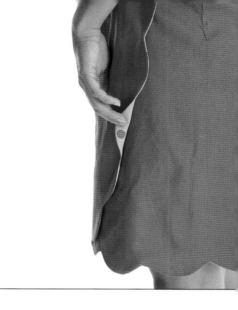

5. **Turn the skirts right side out,** but first trim the scalloped edge using pinking shears. If you do not have pinking shears, use just the tips of your sewing scissors to clip into each curve, taking care not to clip the stitches. Turn the skirt right side out and press. Machine-baste the top waistline edges together.

6. **Sew the waistband.** With the right sides together, stitch the two waistbands together along the top, side, and the first 2" from each end of the bottom edges, as shown. Trim the seam allowance at the corners. Turn the waistband right side out and press. Remember there is a 2" waistband extension on both front edges because the skirt is reversible.

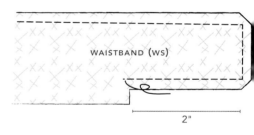

WAISTBAND (WS)

2"

step 6

7. **Attach the waistband.** With the right sides together, pin one edge of the waistband to the skirt with the ends extending past the skirt front edge by 2". Machine-stitch through one layer of the waistband and both skirt layers. Press the seam allowances toward the waistband.

8. **Finish the waistband.** Press the remaining waistband seam allowance to the wrong side and slipstitch (page 29) the waistband closed.

9. **Sew on the closure.** Try on the skirt and mark the hook-and-eye locations on the waistband extensions and inside waistband. Take off the skirt and hand-sew a skirt hook at both ends and an eye at each coordinating mark (page 39).

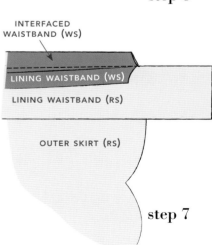

INTERFACED WAISTBAND (WS)

LINING WAISTBAND (WS)

LINING WAISTBAND (RS)

OUTER SKIRT (RS)

step 7

Strong Suit Skirt

Design Variation: Asymmetrical Hemline

For the skirt shown, I drafted two front pieces that mirror each other. If you would like them to be different, simply draft each front piece separately; just make sure the front matches up to the back at the sides so they join correctly.

THURSDAY

Draft the Pattern

1. **Trace your basic wrap skirt slopers** onto drafting paper, but leave room around the front sloper. Make sure the pattern doesn't have any seam or hem allowances included yet.

2. **Lower the waistline** the desired amount on both the front and back patterns (see page 65). Draw design lines for a contoured waistband below the dart points and cut off the waistband (page 67) on both the front and back patterns. Save the waistband pieces and use them to draft the waistbands after shaping the front (step 9).

3. **Draw the front pocket opening** at the side seam and draw the pockets. The pocket opening can be straight, curved, or even a fun shape; it's up to you. Then, draw the pocket bag (or pouch) on the skirt. Make the pocket as deep as you want. Once you are satisfied with the shape of the pocket, flip the pattern over so the center front lines are together and trace the skirt front again to create a whole skirt front. Trace the pocket design lines too.

4. **Draw the front shaped hemline.** For this skirt, the hemline starts ¾" from the pocket opening on the left side and finishes at the opposite side seam, as shown. Make sure to draw the hemline below the pocket bag. Cut off the pattern along the shaped hemline design line.

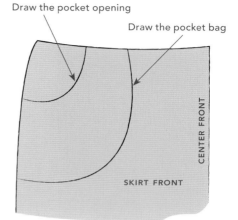

Draw the pocket opening

Draw the pocket bag

CENTER FRONT

SKIRT FRONT

step 3

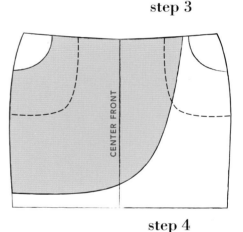

CENTER FRONT

step 4

TIP To eliminate the darts as for the skirt shown, draw the waistband seamline at the bottom edge of the front darts.

5. **Make the two pocket pattern pieces** by tracing them from the skirt front pattern. To make the pocket, you need a pocket backing and a pocket facing. First, trace the pocket backing from the side seam to the outside edges of the pocket bag/pouch and along the top edge. Then, trace the facing from the pocket opening to the outside edges of the pocket bag/pouch. Add ½" seam allowance all around.

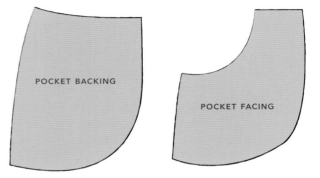

6. **Finish the skirt front pattern** by cutting the front away along the pocket opening; add ½" seam allowance to the pocket opening.

7. **Draft a hemline facing.** Draw a line inside the skirt 2" parallel to the hemline. Trace the new line and the hemline onto separate paper and add ½" seam allowance all around.

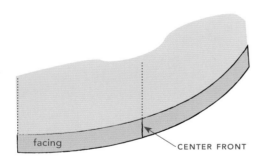

facing   CENTER FRONT

step 7

8. **Draft the skirt back** by adjusting the hemline so that it matches the front at the side seams. Refer to step 7 to make a 2" facing for the back hem. Mark the skirt back to cut the center back on the fabric fold.

PATTERN DRAFTING NOTE

I opted to face the curved hemline of this skirt, which requires drafting a separate hem-facing pattern piece. This hemming technique is shown on page 49. However, feel free to hem your skirt any way you would like.

9. **Draft the waistbands** using the pieces you cut off the skirt front and back in step 2. Lay the front waistband up to the skirt front and cut off the left front edge to match the shaped skirt front. Pin the darts closed on both front and back pieces.

10. **Add ½" seam allowances** to the skirt front and back, including the bottom edge. Because there is a hem facing, there is no need to add a hem allowance, only seam allowance. Add ½" seam allowances all around the front and back waistbands.

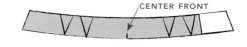

CENTER FRONT

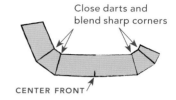

Close darts and
blend sharp corners

CENTER FRONT

FRONT WAISTBAND

step 9

Sew the Strong Suit Skirt

1. **Cut out the fabric.** Use the newly drafted pattern pieces to cut the following:

   - *From fabric:* two skirt fronts, two pocket backings, and two pocket facings, four front waistbands, and two front hem facings. Also cut on the fabric fold: one skirt back, one back hem facing, and two back waistbands.

   - *From interfacing:* one back waistband on the fold and two front waistbands.

2. **Apply interfacing.** Following the manufacturer's instructions, fuse the interfacing to the wrong side of two front waistbands and one back waistband.

3. **Stitch the darts.** If you have any darts in your design, stitch them now. The lower waist and wider waistband in this skirt probably eliminated the darts.

SUPPLIES

> 2¼ yards of 44/45" fabric

> ¾ yard of fusible interfacing

> 2 snaps

> Matching thread

> Contrasting embroidery floss (optional)

> Embroidery hand needle (optional)

DESIGN NOTE

For extra color and design variation, add a running stitch with a hand needle and contrasting embroidery floss after the skirt is assembled. This detail also looks great in a matching color for a subtle bespoke look.

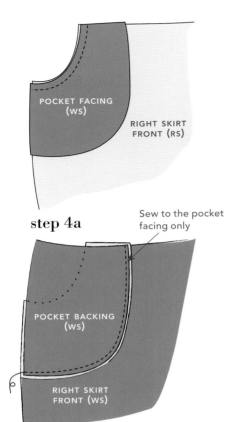

step 4a

Sew to the pocket facing only

POCKET FACING (WS)

RIGHT SKIRT FRONT (RS)

POCKET BACKING (WS)

RIGHT SKIRT FRONT (WS)

step 4b

POCKET BACKING (RS)

SKIRT FRONT (RS)

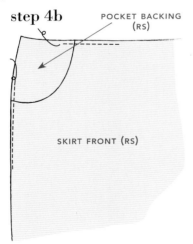

step 4c

4. **Assemble the pockets. a)** With the right sides together and raw edges aligned, stitch one pocket facing to each skirt front along the pocket opening. If the seam allowance is curved, clip into the seam allowance along the curve. Press the seam allowance toward the pockets and understitch ⅛" from the seamline.

b) Turn the pocket facings to the wrong side and press. If you want to edge or topstitch the pocket opening, do it now (see step 8). Then, pin a pocket backing to each pocket facing along the curved edge with the right sides together. Working from the wrong side of the skirt, stitch around the curved edges, taking care not to include the skirt front in the stitching.

c) Pin the pockets to the skirt front at the waistline and side seam edges and baste them in place.

5. **Machine-stitch the skirt** fronts to the back with the right sides together and side seams aligned. Press the seam allowances open.

6. **Assemble and attach the hem facings.** With the right sides together and side seams aligned, stitch the front hem facings to the back hem facing. Press the seam allowances open.

Pin the hem facing to the skirt hem with the right sides together and raw edges aligned. Stitch the facing to the skirt and clip any curves. Turn to page 49 for details on finishing a faced hem.

7. **Assemble and attach the waistband,** as on page 69. Try on the skirt and mark the placement for your snaps with a temporary fabric marker. Take the skirt off and hand-sew the snaps in place.

8. **For the contrast stitching,** thread an embroidery needle with four strands of embroidery floss. Hand-sew around the garment edges with a long running stitch (see the tip on page 28) through the outside layer, and not through to the inside of the skirt.

FRIDAY

Quick Draw Skirt

Design Variations:
Tucks and Lining

Tucks are essentially just folds of fabric or pleats stitched in place from the right side of a garment. They can be drafted to any width and are a cinch to sew. You can make a cluster of them as it was done for this skirt, or create a design with them positioned all over your garment.

Draft the Pattern

1. **Trace your basic wrap skirt slopers** onto drafting paper. Make sure they do not have any seam or hem allowances included yet.

2. **If want to lower the waistline,** draft those changes now following the directions on page 65.

3. **Draft a two-piece waistband** by drawing a design line for a 1½"-wide waistband and cutting it off. Draft the waistband and facing patterns using the cut-off waistbands (page 66).

4. **Plan the tucks.** You can design your tucks so they are horizontal, vertical, or even diagonal. Consider both the front and back of the skirt. Practice folding tucks in your fabric to make sure you like the spacing and width. When you're satisfied, multiply the desired depth (width) of each tuck by two to determine the *tuck intake*. Draw straight lines on the paper for each tuck, spacing them as far apart as desired and allowing for the tuck intake needed for each tuck. Crease the tucks into the paper following the design lines.

5. **Position the sloper front** (from step 2) on top of the tucked paper and trace the outside edges and dart(s). Cut out the pattern and unfold the tucks for the skirt front pattern. Repeat with the sloper back.

PATTERN DESIGN NOTE

Determine where you want your tucks and how deep you want them to be before you draft your pattern. Practice sewing a few tucks on a scrap of your chosen fabric to see how the fabric behaves and how different widths look. This skirt features four vertical tucks on the right front and six horizontal tucks close to the hemline around the entire skirt. The tucks are ½" deep.

step 4

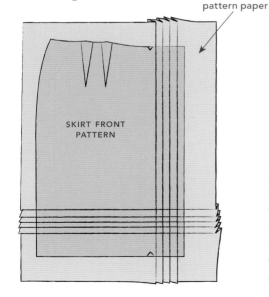

pattern paper

SKIRT FRONT PATTERN

step 5

6. **Draft the lining patterns** by tracing the front and back slopers from step 2, after you have made any waistline changes but before you have added the tucks. Trim ½" away from the center front and back edges, and hemlines of both slopers. Mark these as the lining front and back.

7. **Draft the ties.** For the skirt shown here, the finished ties are the same width as the waistband, but you can make them as wide or narrow as you like. (Finished ties are 1" wide and 32½" and 47½" long. They are different lengths because one wraps farther around the body.) Draft a rectangle to the desired width and length, or measure and cut directly on the fabric (just remember to add seam allowance).

8. **Complete the pattern.** Add ½" seam and hem allowances around all the pieces, including the lining.

Sew the Quick Draw Skirt

1. **Cut out the fabric.** Use the newly drafted pattern pieces to cut the following:
   - *From fabric:* two skirt fronts (if you designed the skirt fronts differently, cut them separately), one skirt back on the fabric fold, four front waistbands, one front left tie and one front right tie, and two back waistbands on the fabric fold.
   - *From lining fabric:* two skirt fronts and one skirt back.
   - *From interfacing:* two front waistbands and one back waistband on the fold.

2. **Apply interfacing.** Following the manufacturer's instructions, fuse the interfacing to the wrong side of two front waistbands and one back waistband.

SUPPLIES
> 2⅞ yards of 44/45" fabric
> 2¼ yards of 44/45" lining fabric
> 1 yard of fusible interfacing
> 2 snaps
> Matching thread
> Temporary fabric marker

3. **Stitch any darts** in the skirt front and back.

4. **Sew the side seams.** With the right sides together, stitch the skirt fronts to the back at the side seams. Mark the tucks onto the skirt using a temporary fabric marker. Clean finish each center-front raw edge with a ¼" double-fold hem, topstitched close to the inside fold.

5. **Sew the tucks one at a time.** a) Fold the first tuck in the skirt with the wrong sides together.

   b) Stitch the tuck along the marked line, or the desired tuck depth distance from the fold, then backstitch. Repeat for each tuck and then press them in the desired direction.

6. **Assemble the lining.** Stitch any darts in the lining front and back pieces. Then, with right sides together, stitch the lining fronts to the back at the side seams. Finish each center-front raw edge as in step 4, or as desired.

7. **Attach the lining.** With the wrong sides together, pin the lining to the outer skirt with the top waist edges and side seams aligned. Baste them together at the top waist edges (the lining should be ½" shorter and narrower than the outer skirt).

8. **Assemble and attach the waistband and ties** following the steps on page 79, making sure to leave a slit in the right side seam of the waistband for the tie to slide through. Hem the skirt and the lining separately using your desired hemming technique, or as you clean finished the front edges (step 4).

9. **Finish the skirt.** Try on the skirt and shorten the length of the ties as desired.

CONSTRUCTION NOTE
Tucks are sewn with the wrong sides together so the stitching is visible from the right side. I used a thread that matched my fabric, but you can use a contrasting one to make your tucks stand out even more.

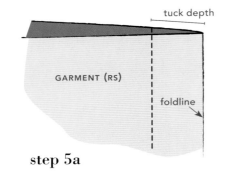

step 5a

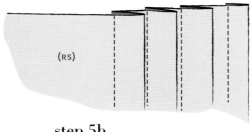

step 5b

Frill
Seeker
Wrap Skirt

Design Variation: Flounces

Flounces are a fun way to add feminine details to any design. They create soft folds and ripples in fabric, but don't add extra bulk like traditional ruffles. You can use them to embellish ready-to-wear, or draft them into your next original design.

SATURDAY

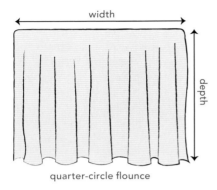

quarter-circle flounce

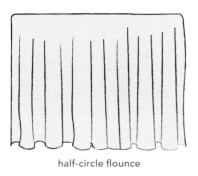

half-circle flounce

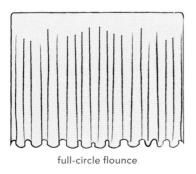

full-circle flounce

step 3

Draft the Pattern

1. **Trace your basic wrap skirt slopers** onto drafting paper. Make sure the pattern doesn't have any seam or hem allowances included yet. Trace the skirt front and back separately and indicate for the skirt center back to be cut on the fabric fold.

2. **If want to lower the waistline,** follow the directions on page 65. Draw a design line for a 1½" waistband as on page 81 and draft the pattern for a one-piece waistband as on page 65. Add ½" seam and 1" hem allowances to all the pieces.

3. **Decide how full you want your flounces.** Most flounces are based on a circle pattern (see opposite page). A full-circle flounce has the most fullness, while a quarter-circle flounce has much less. Determine which fullness you prefer.

4. **Decide how many flounces you want** and where you want them to go. You can have as many flounces as you want and you can attach them anywhere on your skirt. They can vary in depth as the flounces on this skirt do.

   - For each flounce, mark the exact location on the skirt pattern. It might help to trace the skirt front and back pieces on separate paper, pin them together and then mark the desired location(s) for your flounces.

   - To determine the flounce width, measure the length of the marked line (to which it will be sewn). This width measurement + hem and seam allowances will be used to determine the circumference of the inner edge of the flounce pattern.

5. **Decide how deep (long) you want the flounces to be** and add hem and/or seam allowances. This measurement will be the radius of the circular pattern from the inside to the outside. Draw as many flounce patterns as desired (see Drawing Flounces, below).

PATTERN DRAFTING NOTE

Fabric flounces are made from curved pattern pieces that have a shorter top edge than bottom edge. When you straighten out the shorter edge into a straight line, the longer edge drapes into place, creating signature folds.

DRAWING FLOUNCES

You can use a compass to draw your circles, or a trace plate. My favorite way to draft circles is to use a measuring tape, a pushpin, and a mechanical pencil. To do this:

1. Poke a hole at the 1" mark in the measuring tape with the pushpin. Then poke a hole 1" past the desired diameter of the flounce. For example, if you want your circle to have a 4" diameter, poke the hole at 5".

2. To draw, poke the pushpin through the 1" mark and into your paper (on a protected work surface), securing the tape measure in place. Then poke the lead of a mechanical pencil through the second hole in the tape.

3. Draw the circle, making sure the pushpin stays in place and the tape is pulled taught.

If you want to create a very long, very full flounce, you might want to piece several flounces together so you don't have to draft a massive circle. This will also help you save fabric yardage.

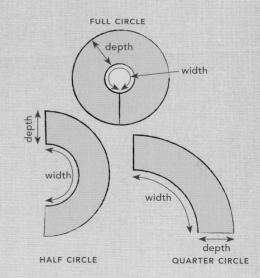

Sew the Frill Seeker Skirt

1. **Cut out the fabric.** Use the newly drafted pattern pieces to cut the following:

   - *From fabric:* two skirt fronts, one skirt back on the fabric fold, four front waistbands and two back waistbands on the fabric fold, and as many flounces as desired.

   - *From interfacing:* two front waistbands and one back waistband on the fold.

2. **Apply interfacing.** Following the manufacturer's instructions, fuse the interfacing to the wrong side of two front waistbands and one back waistband.

3. **Assemble the skirt.** Stitch any darts. With the right sides together, stitch the fronts to the back at the side seams. Then hem the front and bottom edges using your desired hemming technique (pages 45–51).

4. **Prepare the flounces.** If you cut the flounces from smaller pieces to save fabric, machine-stitch them with the right sides together to obtain the desired width. Hem the bottom and side edges as desired.

5. **Attaching piping to the top flounce is optional** (the top edges of the other flounces aren't visible), but it does add a touch of color. You can make your own piping or purchase piping in a variety of colors. Pin the piping to the top edge of the flounce with the raw edges aligned and stitch them together using a piping or zipper foot.

SUPPLIES

> 2⅞ yards of 44/45" fabric

> ¼ yard of fusible interfacing

> 2 yards of narrow, satin-covered piping (optional)

> Piping or zipper presser foot

> 2 snaps

> Matching thread

> Temporary fabric marker

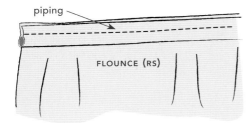

piping

FLOUNCE (RS)

step 5

TIP A narrow hem is most suitable for curved or shaped pattern pieces like the flounces. It also works for the center front and hemline edges.

6. **Attach the flounces. a)** Refer to the flounce location placement lines on the pattern or draw them directly on the skirt with a temporary fabric marker. You can stitch all except the top flounce with the top edge along the desired placement mark and the wrong side of the flounce on the right side of the skirt. Zigzag the flounce in place along the seamline.

b) To attach the top flounce or any flounce that has a visible top edge, pin the top edge and right side of the flounce along the placement line so that the hem of the flounce is toward the waist of the skirt, on the right side of the skirt. Stitch the flounce in place along the seamline. Fold the flounce over the stitching and edgestitch it in place.

note

If the top flounce is piped, use a zipper or piping presser foot to stitch the flounce in place and do not edgestitch it down once you fold the flounce to the right side.

7. **Assemble and attach the waistband** following the steps on pages 68–69. Try on the skirt and mark the desired snap location. Take off the skirt and hand-sew the snaps in place.

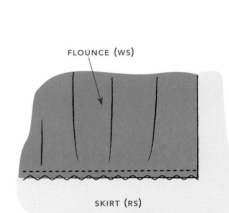

step 6a

step 6b

attaching the top flounce

CONSTRUCTION NOTE
Contrast piping along the top edge of the top flounce hides the raw edge, but you can turn under the top edge if you don't want piping. I left the bottom edges of my flounces raw because I liked the unfinished look, but you can add a narrow hem if you prefer.

chapter 5/
STRAIGHT
SKIRTS

Straight skirts are incredibly sleek, with a narrow silhouette that flatters most figures. Many people credit Christian Dior with pioneering this style with the "H-line" skirts that he designed in the 1940s. Today, the straight skirt, or pencil skirt as it is often called, is perfect for both day and night. It is a clean-looking, tailored garment that's easy to whip up from a basic skirt sloper.

Typically, straight skirts are too narrow at the hem for easy walking, therefore some type of design detail, such as a vent (kick pleat) or slit, is usually added to allow for easier movement. Other design options that allow room for your stride include gathers, godets, and knife pleats. Seven great variations of the basic straight skirt, all with some type of interesting design feature, are featured in this chapter.

Straight Skirt

Draft the Basic Pattern

Your basic sloper (instructions for drafting in chapter 3), without any design changes, is a straight skirt with no flare at the hemline. Since walking in straight skirts can be a little challenging, it's important to know how to add a simple vent or slit at the center back (or front) of a pencil skirt pattern. You can change the location of the slit or vent, depending on your design. Since you don't need to alter the fit of the sloper, all of these straight skirts are super-quick choices for custom-fit garments. This basic straight skirt features a one-piece waistband with a separate facing (see page 65) and center-back vent (see page 121).

Draft the Pattern

1. **Trace your customized front and back basic skirt slopers** on drafting paper, leaving room for design variations and for seam allowance around all the edges, including the center front and center back. Trace the darts onto the paper as well.

2. **Label** your straight skirt patterns.

3. **Design variations.** As called for by one of the projects in this chapter, or according to whatever suits your fancy, add a back (or front) vent or slit (see below and next page). Draft the waistband as directed by the particular skirt design.

Draft a Vent (Kick Pleat)

1. **Plot the length of the vent.** Measure from the hemline up the center-back (or center-front) seamline by the desired amount and make a mark.

2. **Plot the width of the vent.** Draw a horizontal line 2" out from the seamline at the marking.

3. **Complete the vent.** Draw a vertical line from the end of the 2" horizontal line to the hemline, parallel to the center-back seamline. Keep the hemline and side edges square.

note

Once you draft your basic straight skirt patterns, before adding seam and hem allowances, copy them onto patternmaking or drafting paper so you can use them as the starting point for several of the straight skirts in this chapter.

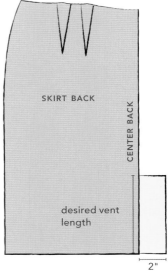

vent / steps 1–3

TIP If the vent or slit is in the center back and you don't want a center-front seam, don't add seam allowance to the center front seam and make sure you cut the fabric on the fold. The same applies to the center-back seam if you want a vent or slit in the center front.

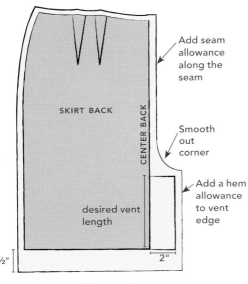

SKIRT BACK

CENTER BACK

Add seam allowance along the seam

Smooth out corner

Add a hem allowance to vent edge

desired vent length

2½"

2"

vent / step 4

4. **Seam allowance and hem.** Add a ½" seam allowance around all the edges, including the vent, and add 2½" for the hem. Smooth out the corner in the seam allowance above the vent, as shown.

5. **Complete the pattern.** Add the same amount of seam and hem allowance to the remaining skirt pattern piece (the front or the back).

Draft a Slit

1. **Decide the length of the slit.** Measure from the hemline up the center-back, center-front, or side seamline by the desired amount and make a mark.

2. **Plot the width of the slit.** Draw a horizontal line 1½" out from the seamline at the marking.

3. **Complete the slit.** Draw a vertical line from the end of the 1½" horizontal line to the hemline, parallel to the center-back seamline. Keep the hemline and side edges square.

4. **Seam allowance and hem.** Add a ½" seam allowance around all the edges, including the slit, and add 2½" for the hem. Smooth out the corner in the seam allowance above the slit, as shown.

5. **Complete the pattern.** Add the same amount of seam and hem allowance to the remaining skirt pattern piece (the front or the back).

note

- -

The process for drafting a slit is the same as drafting a vent, so refer to the same illustrations. The difference is in the width (1½" versus 2"), and they are sewn differently (see opposite page).

- -

SEW A VENT (KICK PLEAT)

1. **Finish the vertical edge of the vent** (both skirt pieces) by turning it under ¼" twice and topstitching the inside fold in place.

2. **Stitch the center seam** (back or front), stopping ¼" below the vent opening. Backstitch to secure the seam. Press both vent allowances toward the left.

3. **Press the vent** along the original seamline (the right vent section extends underneath the left vent section). Using a temporary fabric marker, mark the topstitching line at an angle above the vent, as shown. Topstitch along the marked line, then backstitch or knot the threads.

SEW A SLIT

1. **Stitch the seam above the slit,** stopping ¼" below the slit opening. Backstitch to secure the seam.

2. **Press the seam allowance open** along the seamline, including the slit opening. If you want to finish the edges of the slit, you can turn them under ¼" twice and topstitch the inside folds in place or hand-sew them to the skirt with invisible hand stitches. You can also finish the slit edges with pinking shears or a zigzag stitch, and hand-sew or machine-topstitch them in place. Use whatever technique works best for the weight of the fabric.

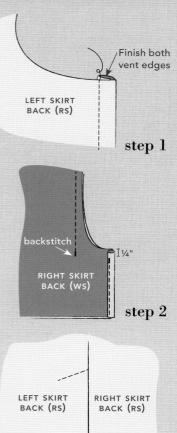

Finish both vent edges

LEFT SKIRT BACK (RS)

step 1

backstitch

1¼"

RIGHT SKIRT BACK (WS)

step 2

LEFT SKIRT BACK (RS)

RIGHT SKIRT BACK (RS)

sewing a vent

step 3

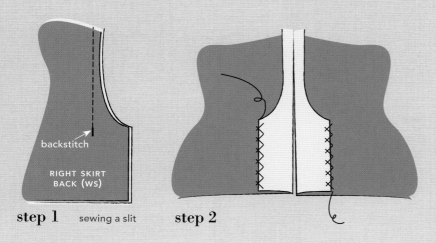

backstitch

RIGHT SKIRT BACK (WS)

step 1   sewing a slit   **step 2**

Sew the Straight Skirt

SUPPLIES

> 1½ yards of 44/45" fabric
> 1 yard of fusible interfacing
> Matching thread
> 7" zipper
> Zipper presser foot
> Hook and eye

1. **Cut out the fabric.** Use the newly drafted pattern pieces to cut the following:

   - *From fabric:* one skirt front on the fabric fold, two skirt backs, and two waistbands.

   - *From interfacing:* one waistband.

2. **Apply interfacing.** Following the manufacturer's instructions, fuse the interfacing to the wrong side of one waistband.

3. **Stitch the darts,** then press them flat toward the center front.

4. **Install a lapped zipper** in the center-back seam (see page 42). If you drafted a center-back vent, follow the instructions on page 121 to sew the vent.

5. **Sew the side seams.** With right sides together, stitch the skirt front and skirt back at the side seams.

6. **Add the waistband.** Assemble and attach the one-piece waistband with separate facing (see page 68). Be sure to allow for a waistband extension above the zipper for sewing on the hook and eye.

7. **Hem the skirt.** Press the bottom edge ½" to the wrong side. Then press it under again by 2". Machine-stitch or hand-sew the hem as desired (see pages 45–51).

Twiggy Skirt

Design Variation:
Button-Front Closure

A front-button front skirt design is a great way to showcase your favorite buttons. This project will teach you how to extend the pattern to accommodate any button size. The skirt shown is made of sports-weight cotton twill, but it would also look great dressed up in a fancier fabric like tweed or washed silk.

SUNDAY

Draft the Pattern

1. **Trace your straight skirt front and back slopers** onto drafting paper, leaving space all around for design features and seam allowances. Change the pattern to a one-dart silhouette in the front (see page 64). Lower the waistline (page 65) and change the skirt length (page 70) as desired on both front and back patterns.

2. **Draft the pockets.** This skirt requires two pocket pattern pieces: a pocket facing and a pocket backing. Draw the pocket opening on your skirt front, following the shape of the innermost dart leg, starting at the top edge and ending at the side seam. Then, draw the outside edges of the pocket bag, making the pocket as deep as you want.

3. **Make the pocket patterns.** Trace the pocket facing and pocket backing onto separate paper to make the pattern pieces as shown. Be sure to trace the dart legs onto the pocket backing piece. Cut away the top corner of the skirt front along the pocket opening.

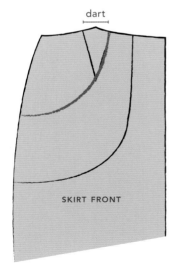

step 2

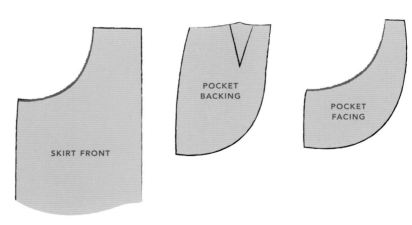

step 3

4. **Plan for buttons.** Measure and record the diameter of the button. Draw the button extension by extending the center front the amount equal to the button diameter.

5. **Draw the center-front facing.** The facing can be drafted as a separate piece, but it's easy to incorporate it into the skirt front. To draft an attached facing, extend the center front again, this time by twice the button diameter. Mark the line between the extension and the facing as the button extension foldline. Then, add ½" hem allowance along the outside edge.

6. **Buttonhole placement.** Draw evenly spaced markings for the buttonhole positions, following these guidelines:

   - Note that the buttonhole on the waistband is horizontal while the buttonholes on the extension are vertical. (You will add the waistband buttonhole later.)

   - Buttonholes should be ⅛" longer than the diameter of the button.

   - Plan for a buttonhole at the waist and the fullest part of the hips. The bottom-most button should end 3" to 4" above the hemline.

   - Mark the vertical buttonholes directly along the center front. Mark the horizontal buttonhole on the waistband to begin ⅛" beyond the original seamline.

   - Remember the buttons will rest at the top of a vertical buttonhole and at the right of a horizontal buttonhole.

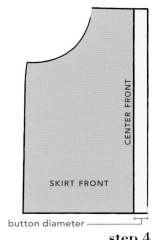

CENTER FRONT

SKIRT FRONT

button diameter

step 4

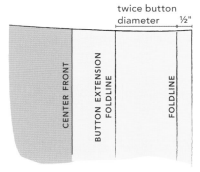

twice button diameter   ½"

CENTER FRONT

BUTTON EXTENSION FOLDLINE

FOLDLINE

step 5

DRAFTING BUTTON CLOSURES

This skirt features a button placket along the center front, with an overlap and underlap for the button and the buttonholes. However, you can use the instructions to add a button placket anywhere on your design (for instance, at a side seam, using smaller buttons). Buttons can be placed horizontally or vertically, as shown.

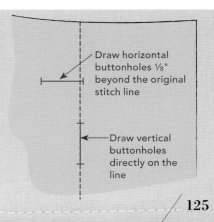

Draw horizontal buttonholes ⅛" beyond the original stitch line

Draw vertical buttonholes directly on the line

125

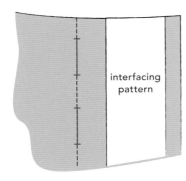

step 7

7. **Draft the button extension interfacing** pattern by tracing the center-front facing. Do not include the ½" hem allowance.

8. **Draft a 2"-wide one-piece waistband** with separate facing (pages 65–66). Keep in mind that you need to extend the waistband to accommodate the new button extension (minus the facing). Mark a horizontal buttonhole (the same length as vertical buttonholes in step 6) in the center of the waistband, starting ⅛" to the right of the original center front and extending toward the side seam.

9. **Add a slit or vent** to the skirt back if desired, following the instructions on pages 119–120.

10. **Complete the pattern.** Add ½" seam allowances to all the pieces (except where it has already been added), including the pocket opening on the skirt front. Add 2½" hem allowance to the skirt front and back.

Sew the Twiggy Skirt

1. **Cut out the fabric.** Use the newly drafted pattern to cut the following:
   - *From fabric:* two skirt fronts with attached facings, two skirt backs, two pocket backings, two pocket facings, two waistbands.
   - *From interfacing:* one waistband and two button extension facings.

SUPPLIES

> 2 yards of 44/45" fabric
> ⅓ yard of fusible interfacing
> Matching thread
> Contrasting topstitching thread (optional)
> 5 buttons, approximately 1¼" in diameter
> Topstitching machine needle (optional)
> Temporary fabric marker

SEWING TIP

Since the buttons and buttonholes are such an important design feature, make sure you practice making buttonholes on two layers of fabric and a layer of interfacing to duplicate the skirt facing.

2. **Apply interfacing.** Following the manufacturer's instructions, fuse the corresponding interfacing to the wrong side of one waistband and the button extension facings. For each facing, position the interfacing ½" away from the front raw edge of the button extension facings on the wrong side.

3. **Stitch the darts** in the pocket backing and skirt back. Follow the instructions on page 106, steps 4–6 to stitch the pockets. Topstitch the pocket opening as desired before stitching the pocket facing to the pocket backing.

4. **Stitch the center-back seam** with the right sides together. If you drafted a center-back vent or slit, follow the sewing instructions on page 121.

5. **Sew the side seams.** Stitch the skirt fronts to the skirt backs at the side seams with the right sides together. Press the bottom raw edge ½" to the wrong side. Then turn and press it under again 2".

6. **Sew the center-front facings.** Unfold the pressed bottom edges. Press the raw edge of both skirt front facings ½" to the wrong side. Fold the facings to the wrong side along the marked foldlines and then refold the pressed hem. Pin the facings and hem the edge in place.

7. **Topstitch** the inner pressed edge of the facing extensions, the outside edge of the extensions, and the hem. Refer to the photograph, pivoting at the hem edge of the extensions to continue the stitching from the top of the extension around the hem and back up to the other extension. This will create two lines of topstitching around the hem.

TIP The distance between the button position and the finished edge of the garment should measure between three-quarters and the full diameter of the button.

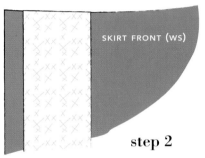

SKIRT FRONT (WS)

step 2

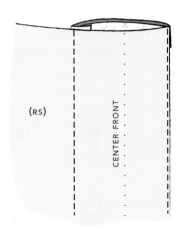

(RS)

CENTER FRONT

step 7

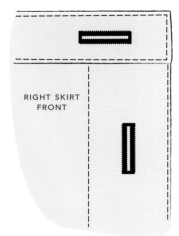

step 9

step 10

8. **Add the waistband.** Assemble and attach the one-piece waistband with separate facing (see page 68). The waistband will begin and end evenly with the edges of the center front overlap and underlap. Add edgestitching as desired.

9. **Sew the buttonholes.** Refer to your pattern and mark the location of the buttonholes on the right skirt front (women's clothing closes right over left). Remember that the buttonhole on the waistband is horizontal while the buttonholes on the extension are vertical. Following your machine's instructions, machine-stitch each buttonhole. To make sure you are positioning the skirt in the machine correctly, sew a practice buttonhole on scrap fabric. Carefully cut the buttonholes open with a buttonhole-cutter, small sharp scissors, or a seam ripper.

10. **Sew on the buttons.** Close the skirt and use a temporary fabric marker to mark the desired button locations on the left skirt. For vertical buttonholes, buttons should be centered in the buttonhole. For horizontal buttonholes, the button should be positioned at the original stitch line (or ⅛" to the inside of the buttonhole). For tips on sewing buttons, turn to pages 38–39.

Great Scot Skirt

Design Variation: Knife Pleats

A knife-pleated skirt hangs straight off the hips, and has a pencil shape when stationary. However once you move, the pleats flare at the hem to allow for a comfortable (and a totally cute) silhouette. These knife pleats are pressed in one direction and are very similar to the tucks featured in the Quick Draw Skirt (page 107). However, unlike tucks, they are not stitched down the entire length of the skirt.

MONDAY

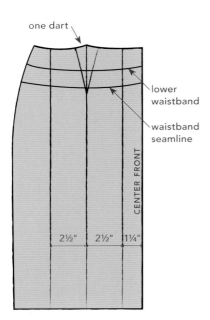

one dart

lower waistband

waistband seamline

CENTER FRONT

2½"   2½"   1¼"

step 3

PATTERN DRAFTING NOTE

To create knife pleats, you will slash and spread the pattern apart at designated pleat markings. First, you'll need to decide how deep you want each pleat and where you want to plot them. The instructions given will produce this skirt design, but mesurements will vary depending on your size.

Draft the Pattern

1. **Trace your straight skirt front and back slopers** onto drafting paper, leaving space all around for design features and seam allowances. Change the pattern to a one-dart silhouette in the front and back (see page 64). Lower the waistline (page 65) and change the skirt length (page 70) as desired on the front and back slopers.

2. **Draft a one-piece waistband** with separate facing following the instructions on pages 65–66 with a ¾"-long extension for a hook and eye at the left side seam. (The waistband shown is 1" wide.)

3. **Draw pleat line markings.** This skirt has three pleats on both sides of the center front skirt. To plot them equally across the front:

    • First measure the skirt pattern width at the bottom of the waistband and multiply times 2 to get the full skirt width.

    • When adding six pleats, you are dividing the skirt into 7 equal sections, so divide the full skirt width by 7. (Example: if the skirt front is 18" across, 18 divided by 7 equals 2.57; you can round that off to 2½").

    • Since you are drafting a half skirt with the center front cut on the fold, you will need to place the first pleat line at *half* the pleat distance from the center front (2½" divided by 2 equals 1¼"). For clarity, the illustration shows these measurements, but yours will be different. Your center pleat may or may not land in the center of the dart, but that is not important.

    • If there is any dart showing below the waistband seamline, measure the width of that dart and save it for step 5.

4. **Slash and spread the pleats.** For this step, you'll need tape and a large piece of patternmaking paper. Cut the pattern apart at the marked pleat line closest to the center front. Tape the center front of the skirt to the paper and spread the remainder of the pattern at the first pleat line by twice the desired pleat depth. (If your pleat depth is 1¾", spread the pleat by 3½".) Continue across for the remaining pleats.

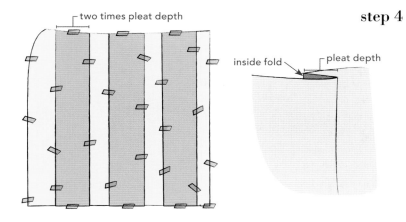

two times pleat depth

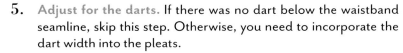

inside fold — pleat depth

step 4

5. **Adjust for the darts.** If there was no dart below the waistband seamline, skip this step. Otherwise, you need to incorporate the dart width into the pleats.

   - Divide the measurement you saved in step 3 and multiply it by 2 (the number of darts in the whole skirt front). Example: if the width of the dart is 1½", then x 2 darts = 3".

   - Divide that number by the total number of pleats (in this case, 6). Example: 3" divided by 6 equals ½".

   - To make the pattern adjustment, divide that amount in half (per the example, one half of ½" is ¼") and shave that amount off both sides of each pleat along the waist. Blend the new pleat foldlines by drawing a smooth curve from the marks to about 4" below the waist.

6. **Draft the back pleats.** Repeat steps 3–5 to draft pleats on the skirt back (if desired).

7. **Complete the pattern.** Add ½" seam allowances to all the pattern edges except the center front and center back, which should be positioned on the fabric fold and don't require seam allowance (page 30). Add 1½" for the hem allowances.

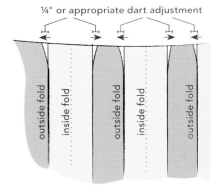

¼" or appropriate dart adjustment

outside fold   inside fold   outside fold   inside fold   outside fold

step 5

TIP You might want to mark a vertical line down the center of the spread sections to indicate the inside fold of the pleats.

> 2½ yards of 44/45" fabric
> ⅓ yard of fusible interfacing
> 7" zipper
> Zipper presser foot
> Hook and eye
> Matching thread
> Temporary fabric marker (optional)

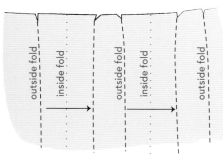

step 3

Sew the Great Scot Skirt

1. **Cut out the fabric.** Use the newly drafted pattern pieces to cut the following:

   - *From fabric:* one skirt front and one skirt back on the fabric fold, two waistbands.

   - *From interfacing:* one waistband.

2. **Apply interfacing.** Following the manufacturer's instructions, fuse the interfacing to the wrong side of one waistband.

3. **Transfer the pleat foldlines** onto the fabric by hand-basting or using a temporary fabric marker. Snip into the end of each pleat fold ¼".

4. **Sew the side seams.** With the right sides together and raw edges aligned, stitch the skirt front to the skirt back along the right side seam. Insert a lapped zipper in the left side seam, following the instructions on pages 42–43.

5. **Hem the skirt** with your desired hemming technique (pages 45–51), or turn the lower edge ½" and then 1" to the wrong side and edgestitch the folded edge in place. It's important to hem your skirt before pressing the pleats.

DESIGN TIP
The pleats can be pressed into a hard crease or left loose to hang freely. Use your design judgment to see what works best for your fabric and silhouette.

6. **Press the pleats.** Following the pleat foldlines you marked in step 3, press the pleats into place. Press lightly for soft folds or press firmly for hard creases. Press from both the right and wrong side of the fabric. If desired, adjust the pleat foldlines at the side seams to hide the seams.

7. **Baste the pleats in place** along the top edge of the skirt. If you want, stitch along the outside folded edge of the pleats all the way or partially down the length of the skirt.

8. **Add the waistband.** Follow the instructions on pages 68–69 to assemble and attach the one-piece waistband with separate facing. Hand-sew the hook and eye (page 39) on the overlap and underlap of the waistband above the zipper.

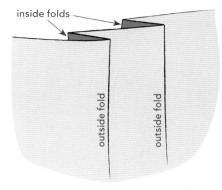

inside folds

outside fold

outside fold

step 6

TUESDAY

High Definition Skirt

***Design Variation:
Waist Stay and Hemline Flare with
Vertical Panels and Godets***

Godets (triangular-shaped fabric inserts)
add a bit of flare to this skirt's hemline.
You can add just one at the center back
for walking ease, in place of a vent or
slit, or you can insert several along the
hemline for extra flare.

Draft the Pattern

1. **Trace your straight skirt front and back slopers** onto drafting paper, leaving space all around for design features and seam allowances. Use the directions on page 64 to change the front and back patterns from two darts to one dart. Lower the waistline as desired (page 65) and change the skirt length as desired (page 70) on both the front and back slopers.

2. **Create eight vertical panels,** or gores. Draw a line from the dart point down to the hemline, parallel to the center front. Repeat for the skirt back. (These four panels will become eight when two of each piece are cut out.)

3. **Cut the front and back patterns apart** along the line. It helps to label the pieces as follows: front, side front, back, and side back. Make note to cut two of all the skirt pieces.

4. **Design the godets.** Decide how long you want the godets to be (for this skirt the godets are 11½" long). Measure up from the skirt hemline at each seam by the desired amount and make a mark indicating the top of the godet. Smooth the dart edges to eliminate any hard corners along the waist seamline.

5. **Draft the godet.** The larger the bottom width of the godet, the more flare the godet will add to your skirt. (The skirt shown features 6"-wide godets.) Draw a triangle using the desired length and width measurements, as shown. Shape and smooth the bottom into a curve. Then add ½" seam allowance to the side edges and 1" hem allowance to the bottom edge.

PATTERN DRAFTING NOTE
Godets can be stitched to the skirt in seams or slits. Ribbon is used as a *waist stay* to finish the waistline, in place of a facing or waistband; it makes for a finished-looking top edge.

CENTER FRONT

step 2

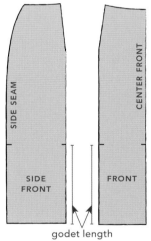

SIDE SEAM

CENTER FRONT

SIDE FRONT

FRONT

godet length

step 4

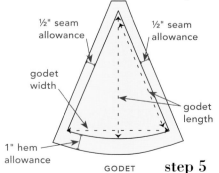

½" seam allowance

½" seam allowance

godet width

godet length

1" hem allowance

GODET **step 5**

SUPPLIES

> 2 yards of 44/45" fabric (see Design Tip)

> 7" zipper

> Zipper presser foot

> Hook and eye

> 1 yard of Petersham ribbon (for waist stay)

> Matching thread

6. **Complete the pattern.** Add ⅜" seam allowance to the top edge of all the panel pieces for the waist stay (see Pattern Drafting Note on previous page) and ½" seam allowances to all the remaining edges. Add 1" hem allowances.

Sew the High Definition Skirt

1. **Cut out the fabric.** Use the newly drafted pattern pieces to cut the following from fabric: two skirt fronts, two side fronts, two backs, two side backs, and eight godets. No interfacing is necessary.

2. **Insert the zipper** in the left side seam or center back (see page 40), and then stitch the rest of the seam to the placement mark for the top of the godet. Backstitch at the placement mark. Press the seam allowance open.

3. **Assemble the skirt pieces.** With the wrong sides together, stitch the two skirt front pieces together along the center front, from the top edge to the godet placement mark, backstitching at the placement mark. Press the seam allowance open. Repeat to join the remaining skirt pieces, including the side seams.

4. **Attach the godets.** With the wrong sides together, pin the godet to the skirt along one godet opening edge, making sure the top of the godet overlaps the opening. Starting at the opening, stitch the godet to the skirt. Repeat for the opposite edge of the godet.

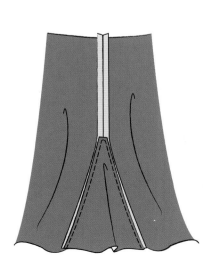

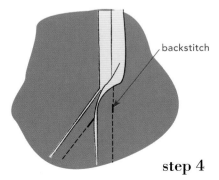

backstitch

step 4

Then, repeat for all the godets. Backstitch at all the seams. Press the seam allowances open on the right sides of the skirt and edgestitch the loose edges of the seam allowances to the skirt as shown in the photo. If your fabric ravels, press the raw edge of the seam allowance ¼" to the wrong side and edgestitch the folded edge to the skirt. If you prefer a more bohemian style or the fabric doesn't fray, simply edgestitch the raw edges in place.

5. **Attach the waistband stay. a)** Start by measuring around the top edge of the skirt and adding 1" for two seam allowances. Cut a piece of Petersham ribbon to that length. Fold both ends of the ribbon ½" to the wrong side. Use your iron to steam a curve into the Petersham.

   b) Pin the wrong side (bottom edge) of the ribbon to the right side of the skirt ⅜" from the top edge with the finished edges of the waist stay aligned with the skirt opening. Stitch the ribbon in place close to the edge of the ribbon.

   c) Turn the entire ribbon stay to the inside of the skirt and press. Machine-stitch or hand-sew the loose edge of the stay in place. Hand-sew the stay ends to the zipper tape. Hand-sew a hook and eye on the stay as shown.

6. **Hem the skirt as desired.** Or, if you have leftover Petersham ribbon, use it as a facing and topstitch it in place. For help on sewing a faced hem, see page 49 and keep in mind that you'll need to trim the hem allowance on the skirt to ½".

DESIGN TIP
The skirt shown here is made of reversible fabric that is orange on one side and pink on the other. To showcase the different sides, I used one color for the right side of the skirt panels and the reverse for the godets. Get creative with your godets by inserting contrasting prints or solid fabrics, or even lace for a flirty detail.

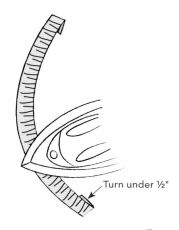

Turn under ½"

step 5a

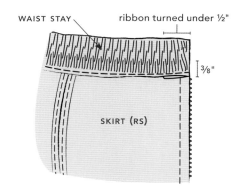

WAIST STAY — ribbon turned under ½"

⅜"

SKIRT (RS)

step 5b

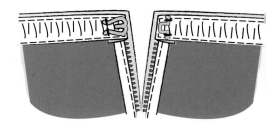

step 5c

Block Party Skirt

Design Variation: Contrast Panels

Dividing your patterns into panels is simple to do and allows for creative color blocking or manipulating stripes in various directions, as was done with this skirt. Use this method to create geometric patterns, or use curved panels for a more organic looking skirt.

WEDNESDAY

Draft the Pattern

1. **Trace your straight skirt front and back slopers** onto drafting paper, leaving space all around for design features and seam allowances. Lower the waistline on both front and back slopers, following the instructions on page 65. Change the skirt length (page 70) as desired on both front and back slopers.

2. **Draft the waistband.** Draft a 1½"-wide two-piece contoured waistband with separate facing, following the instructions on page 67. Eliminate the darts by drawing the waistband below the dart points. Make sure to include a 1" to 1½" extension for the hook and eye above the zipper in the center back.

3. **Design the panels. a)** Decide where you want to add the contrasting panels; you can add them to only the front of the skirt or to both front and back. Also decide the shape of the panels. If you want the front panel designs to continue to the back, make sure the design lines continue through (and align at) the side seams.

   b) Draw the desired panel design lines on the skirt front (and skirt back if desired). Make sure to mark the grainlines on each piece, as well as registration marks at each seamline. If you are not using striped or directional fabric, all the pieces should be cut on the straight grain.

   c) Trace each of the pattern pieces along the design lines. Add ½" seam allowances to the edges of each piece. Add 1½" hem allowance to the pieces that have a bottom edge. If you are using striped fabric or other directional fabric, adjust the grainline arrows to create design interest as shown (see page 141).

PATTERN DRAFTING NOTE

Contrasting panels can be created anywhere on your pattern by adding as few or as many seamlines as you wish. Just be sure to add registration marks to the pieces so you remember how to join them together. It helps to label the pattern pieces too.

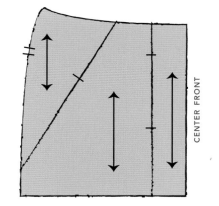

step 3a

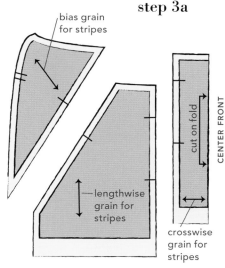

bias grain for stripes

lengthwise grain for stripes

cut on fold

CENTER FRONT

crosswise grain for stripes

step 3b

Sew the Block Party Skirt

SUPPLIES

> 1½ yards of 44/45" fabric

> ¾ yard of fusible interfacing

> 7" zipper

> Zipper presser foot

> Hook and eye

> Matching thread

1. **Cut out the fabric.** To duplicate the skirt shown here, use the newly drafted pattern pieces to cut the following:

   - *From fabric:* one skirt front on the fabric fold (lengthwise grain), two skirt backs (lengthwise grain), two skirt middle front and middle back pieces (crossgrain), two skirt side fronts and side backs (bias), and two front and four back waistbands on the lengthwise grain.

   - *From interfacing:* one front and one back waistband.

2. **Apply interfacing.** Following the manufacturer's instructions, fuse the interfacing to the wrong side of one front and two back waistbands.

3. **Assemble the skirt.** With the right sides together and the registration marks aligned, assemble the skirt front. You can join the smaller pieces together first, or work from the center of the skirt out toward the sides. Press and clean finish (see pages 33–35) each seam. Repeat for the skirt back, if there are design panels. Insert the zipper in the center-back seam (page 40). For help sewing curved seams, see pages 36–37.

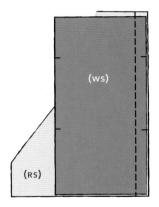

step 3a

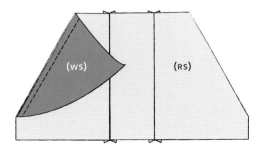

step 3b

DESIGN NOTE

For the skirt shown here, I changed the direction of the same striped fabric for each piece. If you want the stripes to run crosswise or diagonally, change the direction of the grainline arrow before cutting the fabric. (If you are not showcasing striped fabric, all the pattern pieces can be cut on the lengthwise grain.) For even more contrast, try using different fabrics in complementary colors. This skirt has panels in the front and back and features a center-back zipper.

4. **Sew the side seams.** With the right sides together and side seams aligned, stitch the skirt front to the skirt back. Make sure you align any panel design lines at the side seams.

5. **Add the waistband.** Assemble and attach the two-piece contoured waistband with separate facing (page 69). Hand-sew the hook and eye (page 39) to the waistband at the center back.

6. **Hem the skirt.** Press under a ¾" double-fold hem and machine-stitch or hand-sew as desired (pages 45–51).

THURSDAY

New Wave Skirt

Design Variation:
Asymmetrical Darts and
Elasticized Back Waistband

Darts don't have to be simple —
transform them into a stylish
design element. For the skirt
shown here, I topstitched four
asymmetrical darts with contrasting
thread. However, you can sew them
from the inside to hide the stitches.
This technique creates asymmetrical
darts that curve across the skirt front,
from side seam to side seam. To
duplicate the look, you need to start
with a complete skirt front pattern
and then slash and spread it.

Draft the Pattern

1. **Trace your straight back sloper** onto drafting paper, leaving space all around for design features and seam allowances.

2. **Trace the straight skirt front sloper** onto the paper and then flip it over and trace it again with the center fronts aligned to create an entire skirt front sloper. Make sure there is plenty of space around the skirt front to slash and spread the new pattern.

3. **Change the skirt length** (page 70) of both front and back slopers as desired.

4. **Draft separate waistbands** for the skirt front and for the skirt back, since the back waistband will be elasticized. At this point, only draft a skirt front straight waistband with a separate facing as on page 66. Add ½" seam allowances all around.

5. **Plot the curved darts.** Tape the remaining darts closed. Draw four evenly spaced design lines on the skirt front for the new curved darts, beginning at the waistline and ending at the left side seam. Untape the darts and draw a line starting at the bottom of each original dart to the newly drawn design line directly below it. Draw registration marks through each new dart. The illustration shows this completed step.

6. **Slash the skirt front pattern** along the new design lines, starting at the waist and up to, but not through, the side seam edge. Cut through the original darts from the waistline down along the marked line to the new design lines and tape them closed (square up the lines at the top edge). Spread each new curved dart open about 2" at the top edge. Trace the new skirt front so it will be easier to cut the fabric.

7. **Draft the skirt back. a)** To make a wider back (which will be gathered with an elastic waistband), draw four vertical lines equally spaced across the back sloper, parallel to the center back. Measure and make note of the original width of the bottom edge.

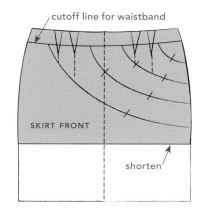

cutoff line for waistband

SKIRT FRONT

shorten

step 5

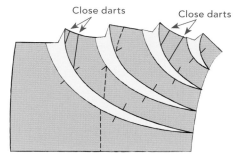

Close darts   Close darts

step 6

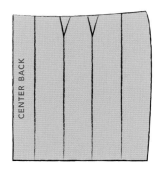

CENTER BACK

step 7a

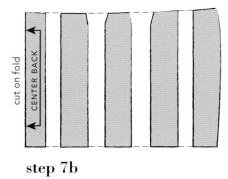

step 7b

b) Cut apart the skirt back along the lines. Spread the pieces evenly apart so that the new bottom width equals 1½ times the original hem width. Tape the pieces onto drafting paper and draw in a new waistline and hemline.

8. **Measure the waistline** (top edge) of the new skirt back. Draft the back waistband equal in length to this measurement, the same width as the front waistband. Add ½" seam allowances to all four sides.

9. **Complete the pattern.** Add ½" seam allowances and 2" hem allowance to the new skirt front and back patterns.

Sew the New Wave Skirt

SUPPLIES

> 1½ yards of 44/45" fabric
> ⅓ yard of fusible interfacing
> 1 yard of elastic (¼" narrower than waistband width)
> Contrasting topstitching thread
> Topstitching machine needle
> Matching thread
> Safety pin
> Pressing ham
> Tape measure

1. **Cut out the fabric.** Use the newly drafted pattern pieces to cut the following:

   • *From fabric:* one skirt front, one skirt back on the fabric fold, two front waistbands, and two back waistbands. Transfer all markings from the skirt front pattern to the fabric.

   • *From interfacing:* one front waistband.

2. **Stitch the darts. a)** Pin the darts from the right side of the skirt, making sure all the registration marks are aligned. Press them all in the same direction, using a pressing ham to shape the curves. Baste across the top edge of each dart to secure it in place.

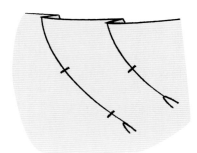

step 2a

b) Use contrasting thread (and a topstitching needle if the thread is heavy) to edgestitch each dart close to the fold. Be sure to keep the registration marks aligned and stitch each dart as far as you like toward the side seam; backstitch so the stitching doesn't come undone.

step 2b

3. **Assemble the back and waistband.** With the right sides together and edges aligned, stitch one back waistband to the skirt back. Press the seam allowance toward the waistband.

   Attach the waistband facing as shown on page 68, step 4. Press the bottom edge of the facing ½" to the wrong side.

   Pin the back waistband facing in place along the waistline seam so it encases all of the seam allowances inside the waistband. Edgestitch close to both the top and bottom waistband edges.

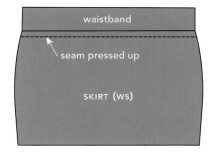

step 3

4. **Insert the elastic.** Measure your total waist circumference (on your body) and divide it in half. Subtract 1" and cut the elastic to this length. Attach a safety pin to one end of the elastic and use it to thread the elastic through the back waistband. Baste each end of the elastic to the side edges of the waistband; this will gather up the back of the skirt.

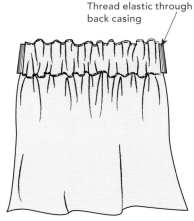

step 4

FABRIC NOTE

I made this skirt out of lightweight chambray fabric and used contrasting thread to really highlight the asymmetrical darts. Choose a lightweight fabric to avoid too much bulk along the back waistline.

5. **Attach the front waistband.** Fuse the interfacing to the wrong side of one of the front waistbands, following the manufacturer's instructions.

   With the right sides together and raw edges aligned, stitch the interfaced waistband to the skirt front. Press the seam allowance toward the waistband.

   Pin the other front waistband (facing) to the front waistband with the right sides together and top edges aligned. Stitch along the top edge, starting and ending ½" from the sides. Press the seam allowance toward the facing and understitch it in place. (See page 68.)

   Press the bottom and sides of the waistband facing ½" to the wrong side.

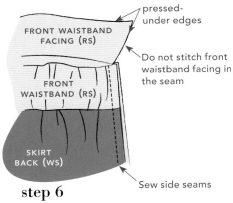

pressed-under edges

FRONT WAISTBAND FACING (RS)

Do not stitch front waistband facing in the seam

FRONT WAISTBAND (RS)

SKIRT BACK (WS)

Sew side seams

step 6

6. **Sew the side seams.** With the right sides together and side edges aligned, stitch the skirt front to the back at the side seams. Do not sew through the front waistband facing.

7. **Finish the front waistband.** Pin the front waistband facing in place, encasing all the seam allowances inside the waistband, including the side-seam allowances. Topstitch the front waistband in place close to the top, bottom, and side edges.

8. **Hem the skirt.** Press under the bottom edge in a 1" double-fold hem, then topstitch close to the inside fold.

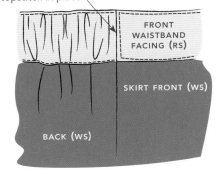

Turn under front facing edges and topstitch in place

FRONT WAISTBAND FACING (RS)

SKIRT FRONT (WS)

BACK (WS)

step 7

FRIDAY

Super Fly Skirt

Design Variation:
Fly Front with Belt Loops

Fly-front zippers may look complicated, but don't let them intimidate you. They're actually very simple to sew with just a few extra steps. Drafting a fly front isn't difficult either, making it possible for you to put together your own unique jeans-style skirt that can be dressed up or down for style and versatility.

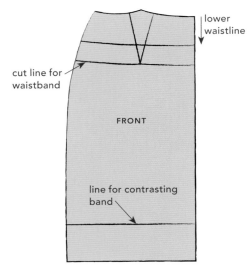

lower waistline

cut line for waistband

FRONT

line for contrasting band

Draft the Pattern

1. **Trace your straight skirt front and back slopers** onto drafting paper, leaving space all around for design features and seam allowances. Use the directions on page 64 to change the pattern from two darts to one dart.

2. **Adjust the waistline and make the waistband.** Lower the waistline (see page 65). Draft three separate contoured waistband pieces with separate facings (see page 67): the left front, the right front, and the back (cut on the fabric fold). Use a curved ruler to smooth out the bend at the closed darts. This waistband is 1½" wide, but you can make it as wide as you want; just make sure the darts end above the waistline seam. To accommodate the fly-front opening, extend the right front waistband 1½" at the center front. Change the skirt length (page 70) as desired on both the front and back patterns. Draft a 3"-wide contrast band across the bottom edge of the skirt front and back.

3. **Draft the pockets. a)** The pockets require two pattern pieces: a pocket facing and a pocket backing. Draw the pieces on the skirt front and then trace them and add seam allowances. The pocket opening can be straight, curved, or even a fun shape; it's up to you. Draw the pocket shape on the skirt as deep as you want.

   b) Once you are happy with the design, trace the shapes onto drafting paper as shown and add ½" seam allowance all around.

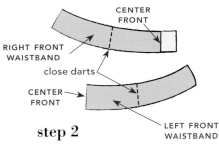

CENTER FRONT

RIGHT FRONT WAISTBAND

close darts

CENTER FRONT

LEFT FRONT WAISTBAND

step 2

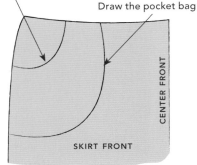

Draw the pocket opening

Draw the pocket bag

CENTER FRONT

SKIRT FRONT

step 3a

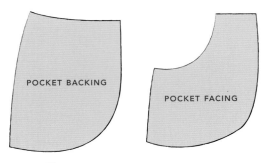

POCKET BACKING

POCKET FACING

step 3b

4. **Finish the skirt front pattern** by cutting the front along the pocket opening (see page 124 for an example). Add ½" seam allowance to the pocket opening.

5. **To draft the fly-front opening** for a 7" zipper, measure 7" down from the waistline on the center front to mark the bottom of the zipper. Draft a fly-front shield that is 2" wide and as long as the zipper. Round off the bottom left corner as shown. The fly shield goes behind the zipper to protect your skin. Draft a fly facing that is 3" wide and as long as your zipper.

6. **Design the skirt back.** The waistline has already been lowered and a waistband drafted (step 2). Draw a design line for the back yoke as desired. The yoke shown here is about 2" wide all the way across, but yours can be as wide as you would like. Add registration marks. Cut off the yoke and tape any darts in the yoke closed.

   To add a vent, follow the instructions on pages 119–120. Don't forget to add a contrast band across the bottom if you added one to the front.

   If your yoke is narrow and there is still dart extending below it, you'll need to omit it. To do this, measure the dart width and shave that amount off the side seam. Blend the side seam so that it curves naturally.

7. **Draft the back pockets** in the desired shape and size. (You can also trace the pockets off your favorite pair of jeans.) Add a ½" seam allowance at the side and bottom edges and a 1" hem allowance across the top.

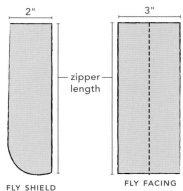

FLY SHIELD   FLY FACING

step 5

PATTERN DRAFTING NOTE

To make a fly zipper closure, you need to first draft a few extra pieces, including a fly facing and shield. Most sportswear garments, such as jeans, have flies that open to the right. For dressy options, such as suit skirts, reverse the directions for a fly that opens to the left.

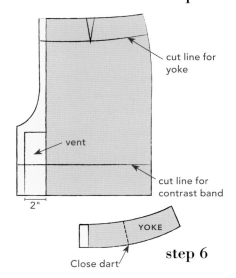

cut line for yoke

vent

cut line for contrast band

YOKE

Close dart

step 6

8. **Complete the pattern.** Add ½" seam allowances to all the pattern pieces except the fly facing, fly shield, and patch pocket (they already have seam allowances). Add ½" seam allowance to the bottom edge of the skirt and top edge of the contrast hem band. Add ¾" to the bottom of the hem band for a hem allowance.

Sew the Super Fly Skirt

SUPPLIES

> 2 yards of 44/45" fabric

> ¼ yard of 44/45" fabric (for contrast band)

> ½ yard of fusible interfacing

> 7" zipper

> Zipper presser foot

> ¾"-diameter button or snap

> Tear-away stabilizer (optional for decorative stitching on back pockets)

> Contrasting topstitching thread

> Decorative thread (optional for decorative stitching on back pockets)

> Topstitching machine needle

> Matching thread

> Tailor's chalk or temporary fabric marker

1. **Cut out the skirt fabric.** Use the newly drafted pattern pieces to cut the following pieces *from the primary fabric*:

   - two skirt fronts
   - two skirt backs
   - two front pocket backings and two front pocket facings
   - two left-front waistbands and two right-front waistbands
   - two back yokes
   - two back patch pockets
   - two back waistbands, each cut with the center back on the fabric fold
   - one fly facing and one fly shield

   From contrasting fabric: Cut two front bands and two back bands.

   From interfacing: Cut one left front waistband, one right front waistband, and one back waistband from interfacing.

FABRIC NOTE
The raspberry-colored denim fabric gives this garment a casual appeal. However, you can make this same skirt from a suiting material for a more formal, office-friendly option.

2. **Assemble the skirt front.** Following the instructions on page 106, steps 4–6, attach and stitch the slanted front pockets to each skirt front. Topstitch as desired. If you created contrasting bands, attach them to the bottom edge of each skirt piece now.

3. **Sew the zipper and fly. a)** Stitch the center front seam from the hem edge up to the zipper marking; backstitch. Clip the seam allowance at the marking (bottom of the fly opening).

   b) Fold the fly facing in half with the wrong sides together. Pin it on the right side of the left skirt front with the raw edges aligned; stitch with ½" seam allowance.

   c) Press the fly facing away from the seam and edgestitch the skirt front along the seam, through the facing.

   d) Finish the fly-shield edges one of two ways: You can sew them together along the long edges with right sides together and then turn them right side out. Or, you can finish them on a serger with the wrong sides together.

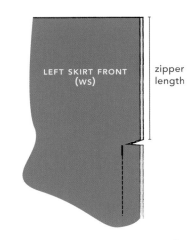

step 3a

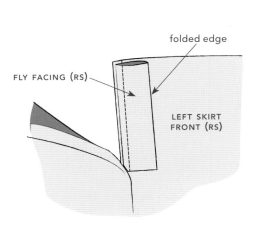

step 3b

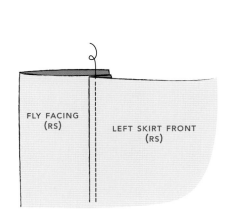

step 3c

step 3d

e) Attach the zipper presser foot to your machine. Place the zipper facedown on the unfinished front zipper edge. Lay the assembled fly shield on top and stitch it in place, along the right side of the zipper tape, as shown.

f) Turn the zipper and fly shield over and press. Edgestitch the zipper in place close to the zipper teeth.

g) From the front of the skirt, pin the fly closed.

h) Turn the skirt wrong side out and stitch the zipper tape to the fly facing close to the right side of the zipper teeth.

i) Turn the skirt right side out and pin the fly closed again; push the fly shield out of the way. Draw a topstitching line on the skirt, using a temporary fabric marker, ¾" from the opening and following the curve of the fly shield, as shown. Topstitch along the line.

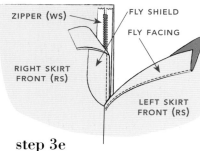

ZIPPER (WS)
FLY SHIELD
FLY FACING
RIGHT SKIRT FRONT (RS)
LEFT SKIRT FRONT (RS)

step 3e

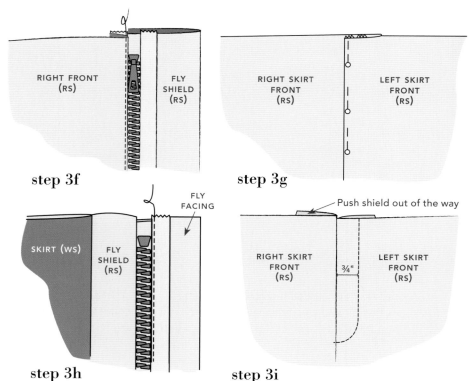

RIGHT FRONT (RS)
FLY SHIELD (RS)

step 3f

RIGHT SKIRT FRONT (RS)
LEFT SKIRT FRONT (RS)

step 3g

SKIRT (WS)
FLY SHIELD (RS)
FLY FACING

step 3h

Push shield out of the way
RIGHT SKIRT FRONT (RS)
¾"
LEFT SKIRT FRONT (RS)

step 3i

4. **Attach the back yokes.** Remove the zipper foot and reinstall the regular presser foot to attach the back yokes. Pin one yoke to one skirt back with right sides together and edges aligned. Stitch in place and repeat for the remaining yoke and skirt back.

5. **Sew the center-back seam.** For help sewing a vent, if you drafted one, turn to page 121.

6. **Assemble and attach the back pockets.** Turn under the top edge of one back pocket ½" twice. Topstitch along both folds. Repeat for the second pocket. If you want to decorate them, do that now.

   Press under the remaining edges of each pocket ½". Position the pockets on the skirt, below the yoke, and topstitch them in place close to the side and bottom edges. Topstitch them again ¼" inside the first stitching.

step 4

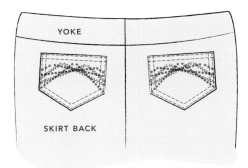

DECORATED POCKETS

If you want to add a design to your pockets, draw it onto the pocket fabric using a temporary fabric marker. Then pin a piece of tear-away stabilizer behind the pocket. Machine-stitch your design onto the pocket. Repeat for the second pocket.

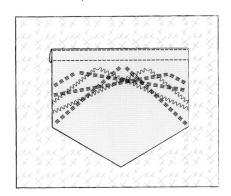

7. **Assemble the skirt.** With the right sides together and side seams aligned, stitch the skirt front to the skirt back.

8. **Assemble the waistbands.** Following the manufacturer's instructions, fuse the interfacing to the wrong side of one left and one right front waistband and one back waistband. Then, with right sides together and side seams aligned, stitch the interfaced front waistbands to the interfaced back waistband. Repeat to join the non-interfaced waistband pieces to make the facing.

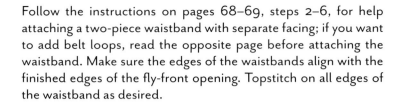

Follow the instructions on pages 68–69, steps 2–6, for help attaching a two-piece waistband with separate facing; if you want to add belt loops, read the opposite page before attaching the waistband. Make sure the edges of the waistbands align with the finished edges of the fly-front opening. Topstitch on all edges of the waistband as desired.

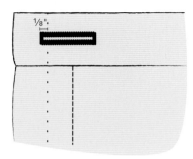

step 9

9. **Make the waistband buttonhole.** Mark a ⅞"-long horizontal buttonhole on the left front waistband, starting ⅛" to the left of the halfway point between the edge of the fly and the topstitching (as shown). Cut open the buttonhole and close the skirt. Mark the desired button location on the right front waistband. Open the fly and hand-sew the button in place.

10. **Hem the skirt.** Press under a ⅜" double-fold hem at the bottom of the contrasting band and topstitch it in place, or hem the bottom of the skirt as desired. In keeping with the design of the skirt, topstitch the hem with a contrasting thread.

BELT LOOPS

Belt loops are quick to make and add a nice finishing touch. Draft them longer for a wider belt.

MAKING BELT LOOPS

1. **Draft a belt loop** equal to the depth of the waistband + ¾" × 1¼" wide. Cut as many belt loops as desired from your fabric.

2. **Fold the loop in half lengthwise** with the right sides together, and stitch the long edges together with ¼" seam allowance. Trim the seam allowance to ⅛" and turn the belt loop right side out. Press. Repeat with the remaining belt loops.

3. **Topstitch,** if desired, along each long edge of the belt loops.

ATTACHING BELT LOOPS

There are two ways to attach belt loops: before the waistband is attached to the skirt or topstitched in place after the skirt is made.

Before Waistband Is Attached

1. **Pin one narrow edge** of each belt loop along the top edge of the right side of the skirt. Baste them in place.

2. **Assemble the waistband as usual,** making sure not to catch the belt loop in the stitching. Once the waistband is complete (including any topstitching), extend the belt loops up and fold under the top edges to match the top edge of the waistband. Make sure you don't lay the belt loop flush against the skirt; add a little bit of room, or ease, so your belt can fit through the loop. Topstitch the folded edges of the loops in place with a narrow zigzag stitch.

Topstitch After Construction

1. **Assemble the skirt completely, including the waistband.** Then, turn under the unfinished, narrow edges of each belt loop ⅜".

2. **Position the belt loops on the skirt** so the edges of the belt loops are even with the edges of the waistband. Topstitch the belt loops in place along the top and bottom waistband edges with a narrow zigzag stitch, adding a little bit of room, or ease, so your belt can fit through the loop.

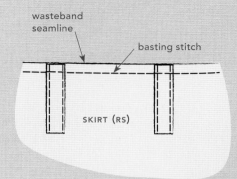

attaching/before, **step 1**

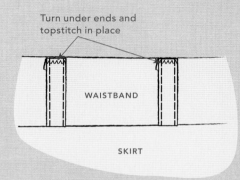

attaching/before, **step 2**

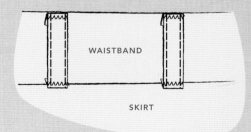

topstitch/after, **step 2**

Velvet Crush Skirt

Design Variation:
Pegged Silhouette and Yoke

Create a pegged silhouette by reducing the circumference at the hemline. This retro style is surprisingly modern when it is made in sophisticated fabrics; it can be a perfect option for day or nighttime looks. Make sure you add a vent (kick pleat) or slit in the back to help you walk in this slim-fitting design.

SATURDAY

Draft the Pattern

1. **Trace your straight skirt front and back slopers** onto drafting paper, leaving space all around for design features and seam allowances. Make the following adjustments:

    - Change the pattern to a one-dart silhouette in the front and back (page 64).

    - Lower the waistline (page 65) and change the skirt length (page 70) as desired on both the front and back.

    - Draw a front and back waistline yoke that is shaped so it is narrower at the side seams and on the back, and falls below the dart point on the front.

    - Draft a center-back vent as explained on pages 119–120.

    - To create the pegged silhouette, make a mark 1½" from the side seam hemline of both the front and back slopers. Make another mark on the side seam of both patterns about 7" below the waist. Redraw and blend the new side seams from the hipline to the hemline.

2. **Add registration marks to the yoke** and cut apart the skirt front and back at the yoke.

3. **Add fullness to the skirt front below the yoke.** Do this by drawing two lines from the side seam to the new top edge of the skirt. Spread each slash line 2" at the top edge to create two 1"-wide pleats as shown. Tape the spread skirt pattern onto paper and even out the top edge of the skirt. You might want to trace the front skirt pattern so it is easier to cut the fabric.

PATTERN DRAFTING NOTE
To draft the pegged silhouette, reduce the width of the hemline at the side seams. Deciding how much to take in at the hemline is a personal preference. You might want to make this skirt from inexpensive fabric to test how narrow you want it, or measure the circumference of a skirt you like.

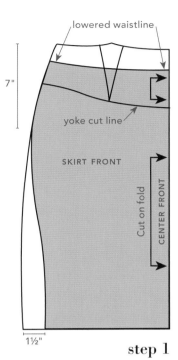

step 1

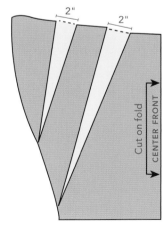

step 3

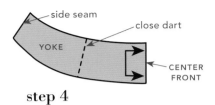

step 4

SUPPLIES

> 2 yards of 44/45" fabric

> 1 yard of fusible interfacing

> 7" zipper

> Zipper presser foot

> Hook and eye

> Matching thread

> Temporary fabric marker

step 3

4. **Pin the darts closed** on the yokes and redraw the patterns, smoothing the top and bottom edges.

5. **Complete the pattern.** Add ½" seam allowances around all the pieces except the center front and add 2" hem allowance to the skirt front and back. Plan for a center-back zipper.

Sew the Velvet Crush Skirt

1. **Cut out the fabric.** Use the newly drafted pattern pieces to cut the following:

   - *From fabric:* one skirt front and two front yokes on the fabric fold, two backs and four back yokes. Transfer the pleat marks onto the fabric with a temporary fabric marker.

   - *From interfacing:* one front yoke and two back yokes.

2. **Apply interfacing.** Following the manufacturer's instructions, fuse interfacing to the wrong side of one front yoke and two back yokes.

3. **Fold the pleats** toward the center front on the skirt front and baste them in place across the top edges.

4. **Attach the front yoke.** With the right sides together and raw edges even, pin the bottom of the interfaced front yoke to the skirt front. Stitch the pieces together and press the seam allowance toward the yoke. (See pages 36–37 for help sewing curves.)

DESIGN NOTE

For the pegged skirt shown, I added a slit in the back to allow for easy walking. However, this skirt would also look great with a center-back godet. For more on godets, turn to page 135.

5. **Attach the back yoke.** With the right sides together and raw edges aligned, stitch an interfaced yoke to the top edge of each skirt back.

6. **Assemble the skirt back.** Stitch the skirt backs together along the center back, inserting the zipper as on page 40 and stitching the back vent as on page 121.

7. **Sew the side seams.** Stitch the skirt back to the skirt front with the right sides together and side seams aligned.

8. **Assemble and attach the yoke facings.** With the right sides together, stitch the two remaining back yokes to the remaining front yoke at the side seams and press the seam allowances open. This is the yoke facing.

   Pin the yoke facing to the skirt with top edges aligned and right sides together. The yoke facing should extend ½" beyond the yoke at each center-back edge. Stitch the yoke to the skirt along the top edges.

   Press the seam allowance toward the yoke facing and understitch.

   Press the bottom and side edges of the yoke facing ½" to the wrong side. Hand-sew the bottom edge of the facing to the bottom of the waistband to enclose the seam allowances, or stitch in the ditch (see tip on page 69) from the right side of the skirt.

   Hand-sew the side zipper edges of the yoke facing in place and hand-sew a hook and eye (page 39) at the top edge of the skirt, over the zipper.

9. **Hem the skirt.** Press the bottom of the skirt ½" to the wrong side and then again 1½". Hand-sew the pressed edge to the skirt with invisible hand stitches (pages 28–29).

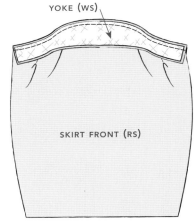

YOKE (WS)

SKIRT FRONT (RS)

step 4

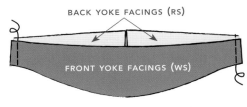

BACK YOKE FACINGS (RS)

FRONT YOKE FACINGS (WS)

step 8

chapter 6
FLARED SKIRTS

Flared skirts camouflage figure flaws while being super cute and comfortable. Depending on your fabric choice, flared skirts can be formal or casual, making each design incredibly versatile.

The basic skirt sloper (see chapter 3) that begins as a straight silhouette is easy to alter into a flared design. Don't worry; adding flare to a hemline is simple. You can use the methods found in this chapter to add a small amount of flare at the hem for an A-line skirt or go dramatic with tons of flare for a fuller shape.

Experiment with each technique and consider making test garments from cheap fabric to see how much flare you like and better assess how much to include in your designs.

Flared Skirt

Draft the Basic Pattern

An A-line is a slightly flared skirt that gets its name from its A-shaped silhouette. A flare added to the hemline of a skirt makes it stand away from the body at the hem, and is flattering to most figures. The "slash and spread" method of pattern drafting adds shape by cutting and spreading the pattern. This basic version features a left side-seam zipper.

Draft the Pattern

1. **Trace your customized skirt front and back slopers** onto drafting paper. Cut out the patterns around the outside edges. On both, start at the outermost dart point and draw a line straight down to the hemline. Make sure the lines are parallel to the skirt center.

2. **Cut and spread the front sloper.** Cut along the line you drew in step 1, from the hem up to the dart point on the skirt front. Tape the center front of the skirt onto paper. Tape that dart closed to spread the skirt open, and tape the spread section in place.

   Measure and record the width of the opening at the bottom of the skirt (x). Then, extend the hemline out past the side seam by half the recorded measurement. Draw the new side seam from the widest hip point to the new extended hemline. Make sure the new side seam and hemline form a right angle (page 59).

3. **Cut and spread the back.** Cut the line you drew in step 1, from the hem up to the dart point on the skirt back. Fold the back dart closed until the skirt spreads open so that the bottom opening equals the skirt front recorded measurement. This will not close the dart completely, as the back darts are typically wider than the front darts. Tape the center back of the skirt on paper and tape the spread section in place.

   Extend the hemline past the side seam as for the front.

PATTERN DRAFTING NOTE

Since you will be cutting and spreading the patterns, trace them onto patternmaking paper without seam allowances and cut them out. Then make sure you have a large piece of paper for taping the slashed-and-spread pattern sections onto. Once you draft your basic flared patterns, before adding seam and hem allowances, copy them onto patternmaking or drafting paper so you can use them as the starting point for several of the flared skirts in this chapter.

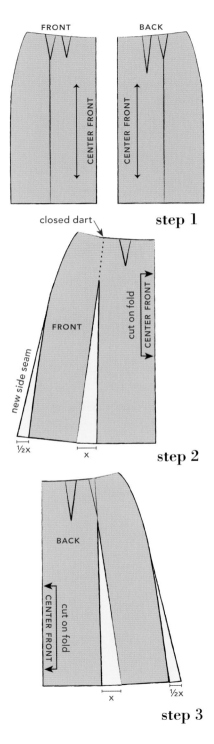

step 1

step 2

step 3

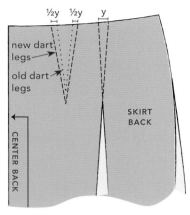

step 3

Measure the part of the back dart not included in the folded dart (y). Make the remaining inner dart larger to include the remaining dart amount, as shown. Erase or cross out the remaining outer dart.

4. **Draft the one-piece waistband** with separate facing as on pages 65–66. The waistband shown is ¾" wide. Any of the waistband techniques work well with this silhouette, so feel free to use the method that you prefer.

5. **Complete the pattern.** Add ½" seam allowances to all the pattern edges, except the center front and center back, which should be cut on the fabric fold. There is a zipper in the left side seam. Add a 1½" hem allowance, or as desired.

Sew the Flared Skirt

SUPPLIES

> 1½ yards of 44/45" fabric
> 1 yard of fusible interfacing
> 7" zipper
> Zipper presser foot
> Hook and eye
> Matching thread

1. **Cut out the fabric.** Use the newly drafted pattern pieces to cut the following:

   • *From fabric:* one skirt front on the fabric fold, one skirt back on the fabric fold, and two waistbands.

   • *From interfacing:* one waistband.

2. **Apply interfacing.** Following the manufacturer's instructions, fuse the interfacing to the wrong side of one waistband.

3. **Stitch the darts and side seams.** Close the darts. With the right sides together and raw edges aligned, stitch the front to the back along the *right* side seam. Press the seam allowance open. Install a lapped zipper in the *left* side seam as on pages 42–43. Be sure to allow for a waistband extension above the zipper for the hook and eye.

4. **Assemble and attach the one-piece waistband** with separate facing as on pages 68–69.

5. **Hem the skirt.** Press under the bottom edge ½" to the wrong side, then press under again 1". Machine- or hand-stitch the hem.

FOR EXTRA FLARE

Use this slash-and-spread drafting technique to add as much flare as desired to the hemline.

1. **Trace the front and back skirt slopers** on drafting paper and cut them out. Be sure to trace the darts on the slopers. On both patterns, start at *both* dart points and draw two lines straight down to the hemline. Make sure the lines are parallel to the center front and center back.

2. **Cut the perpendicular lines,** from the hem up to the dart point on the skirt front along both lines. Tape the center front of the skirt on paper. Tape both darts closed to spread the skirt open at the hem. Tape the spread sections in place.

   Measure and record the width of one of the openings at the bottom of the skirt. Then, extend the hemline out past the side seam half the recorded measurement. Draw the new side seam from the widest hip point to the new extended hemline. Make sure the new side seam and hemline form a right angle.

   Repeat the process for the skirt back.

3. **Balance the patterns.** Put the skirt front over the skirt back so the centers and hemlines are aligned. If the hemlines are not equal, slash and spread the smaller pattern down the center to match the larger one along the hem.

4. **Finish the patterns** as for the basic sloper, steps 4 and 5 on the opposite page.

PATTERN DRAFTING NOTE

For an extra flared skirt, repeat steps 1–3, but draw an extra vertical line between the outermost dart and the side seam so you can slash and spread the sloper even more. Very wide skirts might not fit on folded fabric, which would mean a seam in the center front.

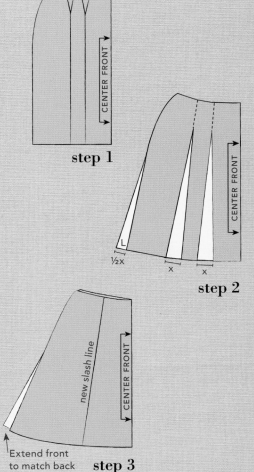

step 1

step 2

new slash line

Extend front
to match back   **step 3**

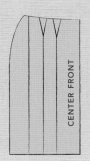

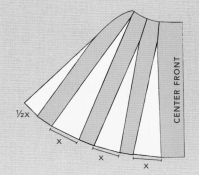

SUNDAY

Girlie Show Skirt

Design Variation:
Full Hemline and Gathered Waist

The following patternmaking method adds fullness to both the waistline and the hemline. Just as for the basic flared skirt (page 162), you slash and spread the bottom of the pattern. However, to create the gathered waistline, you also spread the top edge of the pattern. You will need to tape the pattern to drafting or patternmaking paper as you work.

Draft the Pattern

1. **Trace your customized front and back slopers** onto drafting paper. Trace the darts, but not the seam allowances. Lower the waistline (page 65) and change the skirt length (page 70) as desired on both the front and back slopers. Cut out the slopers around the outside edges.

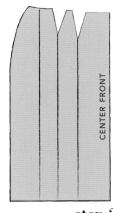

step 2a

2. **Add flare to the skirt front. a)** Starting at the outermost dart point of the skirt front, draw a line straight down to the hemline. Make sure the line is also parallel to the center front. Draw a line from the inner dart to the hemline the same way. Then, draw a third line equidistant between the outer dart and the side seam. If you want even more fullness, add more evenly spaced slash lines. Cut out and discard the darts.

b) Working on a large piece of paper and a mat or board that you can pin into, tape the center front of the skirt front in place with lots of paper to the left of the sloper. Slash the first line from the dart to the hem, but not through the hemline. Secure the still-joined bottom hem edge in place with a pushpin. Then spread the top edges apart the desired amount. The skirt shown here was spread 2".

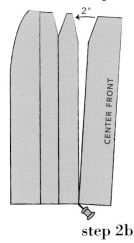

step 2b

c) Transfer the pushpin to the top edge of the second segment as shown. Then spread the hemline by your desired amount. This skirt was spread 4". Tape the edge in place and cut the second slash line as you did the first.

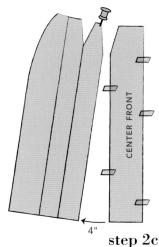

step 2c

PATTERN DRAFTING NOTE

When I was in college, my professor called this technique the "rocking horse" because you pivot the pattern pieces back and forth. You can use this method to spread your pattern pieces apart as far as you like. Experiment and see what works for you and your designs.

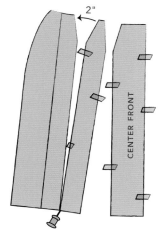

step 2d

d) Transfer the pushpin to the bottom of the second slash line. Then spread the top edge 2" as before.

e) Transfer the pushpin again to the opposite top edge of the second slash line as shown. Spread the hemline 4". Tape the edge in place and cut the remaining slash line from the top edge to the hemline.

f) Transfer the pushpin to the hemline of the last slash line and spread the top edge 2".

g) Transfer the pushpin one last time to the remaining top edge. Then spread the hemline 4". Tape the piece in place. To finish the pattern, extend the hemline 2", or half the amount one slash line was spread at the hem. Draw a new side seam, connecting the new hemline to the waistline. This will eliminate the original hip curve.

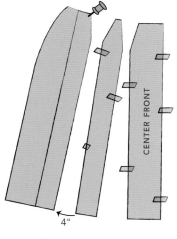

step 2e

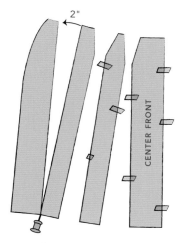

step 2f

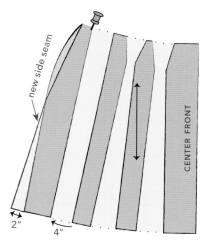

step 2g

3. **Repeat the step 2 process** for the skirt back.

4. **Draft a two-piece waistband** with separate facings as explained on page 66.

5. **Complete the pattern.** Add grainlines and registration marks. Add ½" seam allowances to all the skirt and waistband edges, plus add 1" hem allowance. If your pattern pieces are too wide to cut them on the fold, add a ½" seam allowance to both center-front and center-back edges.

Sew the Girlie Show Skirt

1. **Cut out the fabric.** Use the newly drafted pattern pieces to cut the following (cut all pieces on the fold):

   - *From fabric:* two skirt fronts, two skirt backs, two front waistbands and two back waistbands.

   - *From interfacing:* one front and one back waistband.

note

Larger sizes, or skirts with more flare, may be too wide to cut on the fold. In that case, you will need to add a seam allowance to the center front and center back, and cut out each piece separately. Double the yardage for the skirt for this approach.

2. **Apply interfacing.** Following the manufacturer's instructions, fuse interfacing to the wrong side of one front and one back waistband.

3. **Assemble fronts and backs.** If you cut your skirt pieces on the fold, skip this step. Otherwise, with right sides facing, stitch the front pieces together along the center front, and stitch the back pieces together along the center back.

SUPPLIES

> 1½ yards of 44/45" fabric
> ¾ yard of fusible interfacing
> 7" zipper
> Zipper presser foot
> Hook and eye
> Matching thread

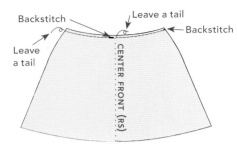

step 4

step 5

step 6

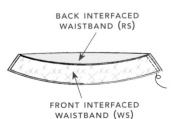

step 7

4. **Make gathering stitches** (page 37). Baste the top edge of the skirt front and the skirt back inside each seam allowance. Backstitch at only one end.

5. **Sew the side seams.** Keeping the basting stitches free of the seam, stitch the skirt front to the skirt back at the *right* side seam with the right sides together. Press the seam allowances open.

   Follow the instructions on page 40 to install the zipper in the *left* side seam.

6. **Gather the top edge of the skirt front** by gently pulling the bobbin thread of the basting stitch(es) from the non-backstitched edge. Gather the edge until it is the same size as the front waistband, and knot off the thread. Distribute the gathers evenly across the skirt front. Repeat for the skirt back.

7. **Sew the waistband.** With the right sides together, stitch the interfaced waistband pieces together at the right side seam.

   Assemble and attach the one-piece waistband with separate facing and extension at the left side seam as on pages 68–69. Add a hook and eye (page 39) above the zipper.

8. **Hem the skirt.** Press under a ½" double-fold hem and topstitch in place, or hem the skirt as desired (pages 45–51).

CONSTRUCTION NOTES

The top edge of the skirt is gathered before the waistband is attached. It's a good idea to gather the front and back separately so that you don't run the risk of breaking the gathering threads. If your skirt is very full at the top, you might even consider gathering the skirt in four sections. This skirt has a zipper in the left side seam.

Lone Star Skirt

Design Variation:
Sheer Overlay and Longer Underlay

I love layering fabrics over one another.
You can soften a bright print with a
sheer solid, or add contrast with an
unexpected under-layer. You can even
use this method to create a lace layer
over a lining. Go to the fabric store
and play with stacking swatches. You
may be surprised at all the fun fabric
combinations that are at your disposal.

MONDAY

Draft the Pattern

PATTERN
DRAFTING NOTE
Some designers feel it
is beneficial to create
an underlay pattern that
is different in size from
the overlay. I typically
do not draft separate
patterns. Instead, I mark
the variations on one
pattern piece (see step 4
at right). However, if
you find it easier, you can
draft separate pieces.
Just make sure you clearly
label all the pattern pieces.

1. **Trace your basic flared skirt patterns** (pages 163–164) onto drafting paper. Do not include seam or hem allowances yet. Trace the darts and lower the waistline (page 65), if desired. Plan for a center-back zipper.

2. **Make the waistband.** Draft a two-piece contoured waistband (page 67) that is wide enough for the design line to be below the darts (the waistband shown is about 2½" wide), but do not add seam allowances yet. Use a curved ruler to smooth out the bend where the darts have been closed.

3. **Draft the ruched waistband.** As with the Spring-Loaded Wrap Skirt on page 91, this skirt has a gathered waistband that is drafted wider than the underlying waistband, gathered top to bottom, and stitched on top of the outer waistband. To draft it, follow the instructions on page 92, step 4.

4. **Draft the underlay** (optional; see Pattern Drafting Note). For most lined skirts, the hemline of the outer layer should be about ¼" longer than the lining. However, if you want the underlay to peek out the bottom, make it longer than the overlay. (The underlay of this skirt is 2" longer than the outerlay.) Clearly mark the different hemline cutting lines, especially if your layers have drastically different hem allowances.

   Depending on the weight of your fabrics, you might want to make the overlay wider at the hem than the underlay. To do this, extend the side seam at the bottom/hem edge of the skirt between 1" to 2" out from the original side seam. Do this on both the front and back slopers. Connect the new hemline to the original waistline by drawing new side seams.

5. **Complete the pattern.** Add ½" seam allowances and ½" hem allowances. Add grainlines and registration marks to all of your pattern pieces (page 72).

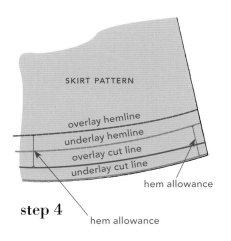

SKIRT PATTERN

overlay hemline
underlay hemline
overlay cut line
underlay cut line

hem allowance

step 4

hem allowance

Sew the Lone Star Skirt

1. **Cut out the fabric.** Use the newly drafted pattern pieces to cut the following:

   - *From overlay fabric:* one skirt front and one front ruched waistband on the fabric fold, two skirt backs, and two back ruched waistbands.

   - *From underlay fabric:* one skirt front on the fabric fold, two front waistbands on the fabric fold, two back skirts and four back waistbands.

   - *From interfacing:* one front waistband and two back waistbands.

2. **Assemble the skirt overlay.** Stitch the overlay pieces together at the side seams using French seams (page 31) and stitch the center-back seam, leaving the zipper area unstitched.

3. **Assemble the underlay.** Stitch the front to the back underlay along the side seams with the right sides together, using traditional seams. Stitch the center-back seam, but leave the zipper area unstitched.

4. **Join the underlay to the overlay.** Pin the wrong side of the overlay to the right side of the underlay at the top edges. Make sure the side seams are aligned. Baste them together along the top edges, using a ¼" seam allowance. Hand-baste the layers together along both sides of the zipper opening.

SUPPLIES

> **2 yards of 44/45" sheer overlay fabric**

> **2 yards of 44/45" underlay fabric**

> **½ yard of fusible interfacing**

> **7" zipper**

> **Zipper presser foot**

> **Hook and eye**

> **Matching thread**

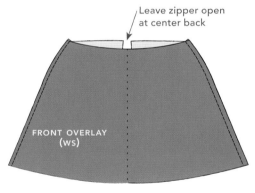

Leave zipper open at center back

FRONT OVERLAY (ws)

step 2

CONSTRUCTION NOTE

When making a skirt with an overlay, you basically sew the two skirts (overlay and underlay) together at the top edges. For the sheer overlay shown here, I used French seams (see page 31) to finish the inside side edges.

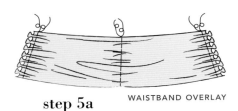

step 5a

WAISTBAND OVERLAY

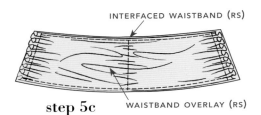

INTERFACED WAISTBAND (RS)

WAISTBAND OVERLAY (RS)

step 5c

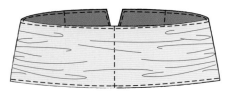

step 5d

5. **Assemble the waistband. a)** Run basting stitches along the short ends of each of the ruched waistband pieces and at the center front of the front ruched waistband; backstitch at one end of each row of basting. Pull the bobbin thread to gather and reduce the width of the overlays until they are the same width as the underlying waistband pieces. Knot to secure the threads.

b) Following the manufacturer's instructions, attach interfacing to the wrong side of one front and two back underlying waistband pieces.

c) Pin a gathered overlay to a corresponding interfaced waistband with the wrong side of the overlay on the right side of the waistband and with the raw edges aligned. Baste around the edges to secure the layers together.

d) With the right sides together and side seams aligned, stitch the assembled waistband pieces together at the side seams. Repeat for the remaining waistband facing pieces.

6. **Attach the waistband.** Pin the gathered waistband and facing to the skirt along the top edge with right sides together and side seams aligned. Stitch them together along the top, and press the seam allowance toward the waistband and press the waistband up and away from the skirt.

7. **Install a centered zipper** in the back seam, following the instructions on page 40. Align the top of the zipper tape with the top of the waistband to install the zipper in the waistband and the skirt opening, through both fabric layers.

8. **Attach the waistband facing.** With the right sides together and side seams aligned, pin the waistband facing to the waistband along the top edges, with the facing extending beyond the zipper ½" on each side of the center back. Stitch in place along the top edge. Press the seam allowance toward the facing and understitch it in place.

   Press the seam allowance along the center backs and bottom edge of the facing to the wrong side and turn the waistband facing to the inside of the skirt. Slipstitch the pressed edges to the zipper tape and bottom of the waistband.

9. **Add a hook and eye** (page 39) inside the skirt at the top of the zipper.

10. **Hem the skirt.** Make a narrow hem (page 48) on both the overlay and underlay.

Line-by-Line Skirt

Design Variation:
Flared Vertical Panels

In fashion design, vertical panels are referred to as gores. The straight skirt on page 134 features gores with godets at the hem. If you would like to add panels to your skirt, but also want the hemline to have more flare than a straight skirt, a few more steps are necessary. The flare needs to be drafted into each panel as shown in the next pages.

TUESDAY

Draft the Pattern ·

1. **Trace the front and back slopers onto drafting paper.** Do not add seam or hem allowances, but do trace the darts.

2. **Draft the gores on the skirt front. a)** At the inner darts, draw a line parallel to the center from the dart point to the hem. Label each segment with a number as shown.

   b) Measure the width of the outer front dart (x) and increase the width of the inner dart by the measurement. This eliminates the need for the outer dart (you can cross it out so you don't get confused).

   c) At the hemline of the skirt front, measure and mark 1½" on both sides of the drawn design line (step 1). With a yardstick or ruler, draw two new design or "gore" lines connecting the dart point to the new marks at the hem. Then extend the hemline at the side seam 1½". Draw a new side seam as shown, connecting the fullest part of the hip to the hem.

step 2a

step 2b

step 2c

PATTERN DRAFTING NOTE

The basic sloper (see chapter 3) works as a starting point for this skirt. However, if you would like to add more flare, start with the flared pattern or a pattern that has already been transformed into an A-line shape, following the directions on pages 163–164.

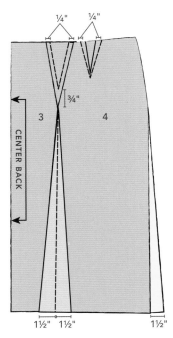

step 3

3. **Draft the skirt back.** On the skirt back sloper, redraw the inner dart so it is a total of ½" wider and ¾" longer. Redraw the outer dart so it is ½" smaller (take ¼" off each side). Then, follow step 2 to draw two new gore lines.

4. **Trace the four new pattern pieces** onto drafting paper following the new gore lines. You can't cut out the pattern pieces because they overlap at the gore lines. Refer to the illustration below for help knowing how to cut the pieces.

5. **Complete the pattern.**
    - Add the grainlines and registration marks.
    - Add ⅜" seam allowances to the top edges of the gores and ½" seam allowances to all the other edges.
    - Add 2" hem allowances to each piece.
    - No waistband is necessary since the top edge of the skirt is finished with a waist stay.

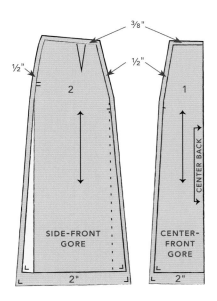
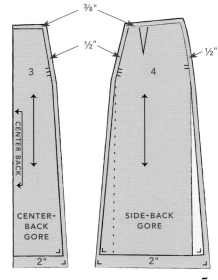

step 5

Sew the Line-by-Line Skirt

1. **Cut out the fabric.** Use the newly drafted pattern pieces to cut the following from both the main fabric and the lining fabric: one skirt center front (#1) and skirt center back (#3) on the fabric fold, two side fronts (#2) and two side backs (#4).

2. **Assemble the skirt front and back.** With the right sides together and raw edges aligned, stitch the center front gore to the side front gores. Press the seam allowances open. Repeat with the center-back gore and side back gores.

   With the right sides together and side seams aligned, stitch the right side seam.

3. **Install the zipper.** Referring to pages 42–43, prepare and stitch the left side seam, and install a lapped zipper.

SUPPLIES

> 1½ yards of 44/45" fabric
> 1½ yards of 44/45" lining
> 1 yard of Petersham ribbon for waist stay
> 7" zipper
> Zipper presser foot
> Hook and eye

SIDE FRONT GORE (RS)

CENTER FRONT (WS)

step 2

step 3

4.   **Assemble the lining.** Repeat step 2 to assemble the lining, leaving the zipper area unstitched.

5.   **Attach the lining.** Press the lining seam allowance along the zipper opening to the wrong side. Then, with the wrong sides together, gore seams aligned, and top edges aligned, baste the lining to the skirt along the top edge. Slipstitch (page 29) the pressed edge of the lining to the zipper.

6.   **To finish the top edge,** cut a waist stay from Petersham ribbon and attach it as for the High Definition Skirt on page 137, step 5.

7.   **Hem the skirt.** For the lining, press under a 1" double-fold hem and topstitch the hem in place. For the skirt, press under the hem ½", then 1½"; hand-sew or machine-blindstitch in place (page 48).

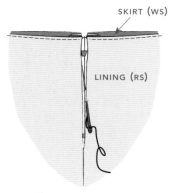

SKIRT (WS)

LINING (RS)

step 5

DESIGN NOTE

This skirt features a lining and a stay to finish the waistline. If you would rather add a waistband, turn to pages 65–69 for how to draft and sew one.

Heavy Metal Skirt

WEDNESDAY

Design Variation:
Inverted Box Pleats

Box pleats aren't reserved for cheerleader uniforms anymore. Here they are inverted and transformed into a chic detail, showcased in modern metallic fabric and a short hemline. Like most pleats, box pleats can be pressed into a hard crease or left unstitched for a softer, less tailored look.

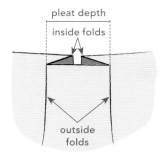

pleat depth

inside folds

outside folds

BOX PLEAT

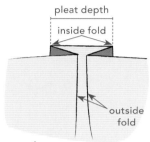

pleat depth

inside fold

outside fold

step 4   INVERTED BOX PLEAT

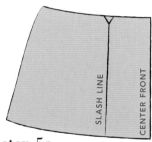

SLASH LINE

CENTER FRONT

step 5a

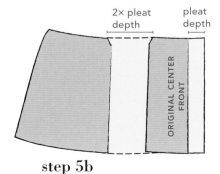

2× pleat depth   pleat depth

ORIGINAL CENTER FRONT

step 5b

Draft the Pattern

1. **Trace your basic flared skirt front and back patterns** (pages 163–164) on drafting paper. Do not include seam or hem allowances yet and leave space all around for design features. Trace the darts. The skirt has a center-back zipper.

2. **Lower the waistline** (page 65) and shorten or lengthen the skirt (page 70) as desired.

3. **Make the waistband.** Draft a 2½"- to 3"-wide contoured waistband with separate facings (page 67). Plan a waistband extension for a center-back zipper.

4. **Plan the pleats.** Determine how many pleats you want and how deep they should be; the pleats in this skirt are 3" deep and inverted (see Pattern Drafting Note below). There is one center front pleat and two additional pleats, each 3" away from the center toward the side seams. There are no pleats in the back.

5. **Draft the pleats. a)** Draw a slash line from the dart point down to the hemline parallel to the center front for the two side front pleats.

   b) Cut the pattern apart on the slash line and tape the center front section to patternmaking paper with plenty of paper on both sides. Spread the side of the skirt away from the center twice the determined pleat depth and tape it in place. Then extend the center front equal to the determined pleat depth.

PATTERN DRAFTING NOTE

Box pleats are easy to add to any design by simply bringing two folds of fabric together. They can be drafted so the folds meet on the wrong side of the garment for traditional box pleats, or with the folds meeting on the right side of the garment to make inverted pleats, as done with this skirt.

6. **Mark the pleat folds** with small clips into the seam allowance. Or, you can mark the inside and outside foldlines the entire length of the pattern, so you can transfer them to the fabric and make it easier to fold the fabric.

7. **Complete the pattern.** Add ½" seam allowances to all of your pattern pieces. Add 2" hem allowance. Add grainlines, note to cut the front on the fabric fold, and add registration marks.

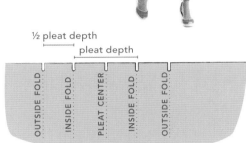

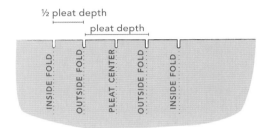

step 6, box pleat

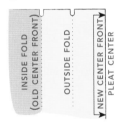

step 6, inverted box pleat

Sew the Heavy Metal Skirt

1. **Cut out the fabric.** Use the newly drafted pattern pieces to cut the following:

   • *From fabric:* one front skirt and two front waistbands on the fabric fold, and two skirt backs and four back waistbands.

   • *From interfacing:* one front and two back waistbands.

SUPPLIES

> 1½ yards of 44/45" fabric
> ¾ yard of fusible interfacing
> 7" zipper
> Zipper presser foot
> Hook and eye

2. **Apply interfacing.** Following the manufacturer's instructions, fuse interfacing to the wrong side of each waistband.

3. **Fold the pleats.** Refer to the registration marks to fold the pleats in the skirt front and pin them in place across the top edge. Baste across the top edge.

4. **Insert the zipper.** With the right sides together and raw edges aligned, insert the zipper (page 40) and stitch the center-back seam.

5. **Sew the side seams.** With the right sides together, stitch the skirt front and back together along the side seams.

6. **Assemble and attach the waistband.** With the right sides together and raw edges aligned, stitch the two interfaced back waistbands to the interfaced front waistband at the side seams.

   Refer to pages 68–69 for how to assemble and attach a two-piece waistband and facing with a waistband extension.

7. **Hem the skirt.** Carefully press under the lower edge of the skirt ½" to the wrong side, and then press under 1½". Topstitch close to the inner folded edge, or sew the hem as desired (pages 45–51).

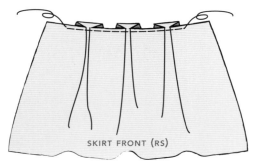

SKIRT FRONT (RS)

step 3

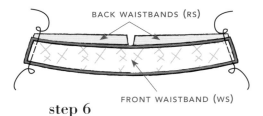

BACK WAISTBANDS (RS)

FRONT WAISTBAND (WS)

step 6

FABRIC NOTE

This skirt is made of a metallic, floral-print fabric. Though the end result is wonderful, pressing metallic fabrics can be tricky. Always use a press cloth between the fabric and the iron and lower the heat setting to prevent damage to the fibers.

Piece Gathering Skirt

Design Variation:
Ruched Panels and Faced Waistline

Gathered panels are a snap to draft, and can be added anywhere on any skirt. The waistline on this skirt is finished with a facing instead of a waistband. A facing is a separate pattern piece that is sewn to the garment's edge and turned toward the inside, for a neatly finished edge.

THURSDAY

Draft the Pattern

1. **Trace your basic flared skirt front and back pattern** (page 163) onto drafting paper. Do not include seam or hem allowances yet and leave space all around for design features. Trace the darts.

2. **Waistline and facing.** Lower the waistline (page 65) and lengthen or shorten the skirt (page 70) as desired. Instead of a waistband, draft a facing to finish the skirt waistline (also on page 70). Start by pinning any remaining darts closed.

   Trace the top edge of the skirt front and back, and for 2½" down the side seam and center front. Connect the lines. Trace the drafted facing (do not cut it off). Indicate that the center front of the skirt and facing should be cut on the fabric fold.

3. **Plan the gathered panel.** Decide the shape and location for the panel and draw the design lines on the skirt front. If you want the panel to extend to the back of the skirt, position the skirt back next to the skirt front so the side seams are together and draw continuous design lines from the front to the back. Add registration marks (page 72).

4. **Cut away the panel pieces** from both the front and back skirt patterns and tape them together at the side seam.

5. **Slash and spread the panel** the desired amount by drawing vertical lines, cutting them, and spreading the pattern. Tape the spread

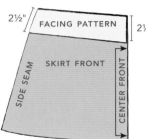

step 2

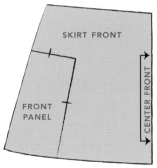

step 3

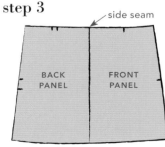

step 4

PATTERN DRAFTING NOTE

Create gathered panels by slashing and spreading a specific area within a pattern. Simply decide where you want to add the gathered, or ruched, detail, then slash and spread the piece as much as you would like. Trace the new pattern and add registration marks so you'll be able to sew the fabric pieces together.

panel pieces on drafting or patternmaking paper and trace over them to create the pattern piece. (For this skirt, the panels were spread 2½ times the original width.)

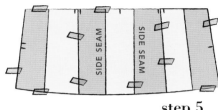

6. **Complete the pattern.** Add grainlines; the skirt front is cut on the fabric fold and an invisible zipper is installed in the center-back seam. Add ½" seam allowances to all edges, including the panel edges. Add 2" hem allowance.

Sew the Piece Gathering Skirt

1. **Cut the fabric.** Use the newly drafted pattern pieces to cut the following:

    *   *From fabric:* one skirt front and one front facing on the fold, two skirt backs, two back facings, and two side panels.

    *   *From interfacing:* one front facing on the fold and two back facings.

2. **Apply interfacing.** Following the manufacturer's instructions, fuse the interfacing to the wrong side of each facing.

3. **Install the zipper.** Stitch the center-back seam with the right sides together and insert the invisible zipper (see page 41).

4. **Assemble the skirt.** With the right sides together and raw edges aligned, stitch the skirt back to the skirt front at the side seams.

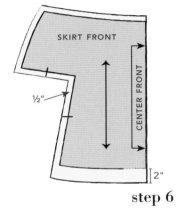

step 6

SUPPLIES

> 1¾ yards of 44/45" fabric
> ¾ yard of fusible interfacing
> 7" invisible zipper (regular zipper works too)
> Invisible zipper presser foot
> Hook and eye
> Matching thread

CONSTRUCTION NOTE

You can make the gathered panels from the same fabric as the body of the skirt, or a contrasting fabric. Be sure to stitch the skirt side seams before attaching the panels.

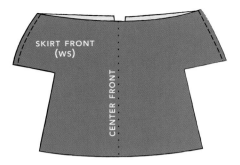

step 4

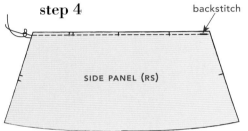

step 5

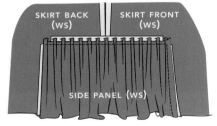

step 6a

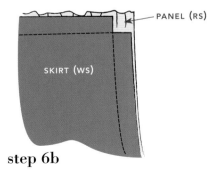

step 6b

5. **Gather the panels** by running one or two rows of basting stitches across the top edge of each side panel. Backstitch at one end.

6. **Attach the panels. a)** Pull the bobbin basting thread on one skirt panel to gather it until it matches the skirt opening. Pin the side and top edges of the panel to the skirt opening with the right sides together and raw edges aligned.

   b) For help on sewing corners, see pages 35–36. Stitch the panel to the skirt.

7. **Assemble and attach the facing.** With the right sides together and raw edges aligned, stitch the two back facings to the front facing at the side seams. Press under the center-back edges of the facing ½" to the wrong side.

   Stitch the facing to the top edge of the skirt with the right sides together and raw edges aligned (pressed side edges align with zipper opening).

   Press the seam allowance toward the facing and understitch it in place (page 37). Hand-sew the facing to the zipper tape at the center-back edge, and hand-tack it at each side seam. Sew a hook and eye (page 39) above the zipper.

8. **Hem the skirt.** Press under the lower edge of the skirt ½" to the wrong side and then press under 1½". Topstitch close to the inner folded edge, or sew the hem as desired (pages 45–51).

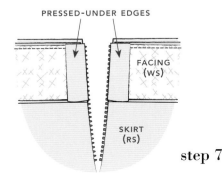

step 7

FRIDAY

New Twist Skirt

Design Variation: Twisted Bubble Hemline

Bubble hems are turned under at the bottom of the skirt and attached to a lining, or stay, to create a soft fold and a "bubbled" silhouette. For a more dramatic bubble, draft more fullness and use a stiffer fabric than the skirt shown here. For a more draped look, choose a lighter fabric that falls closer to the body. This bubble hem is twisted for a different take on the design, but you can keep yours straight, if you prefer.

Draft the Pattern

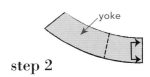

yoke

step 2

1. **Trace your basic flared skirt front and back pattern** (page 163) onto drafting paper. Do not add any seam or hem allowances yet, but do trace the darts.

2. **Waistline and yoke.** Lower the waistline (page 65) as desired on both front and back slopers. Draft a yoke design line on both slopers that meets at the side seams and is below the dart points. The yoke shown here is 3" wide. Plan for a zipper in the left side seam.

   Once you like the shape of the yoke, add registration marks (page 72) along the top and side seams, and cut it off along the seamline. Tape the darts on the yokes closed and smooth out any rough corners along the top and bottom edges.

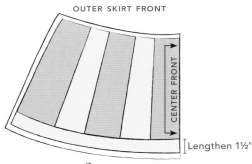

OUTER SKIRT FRONT

CENTER FRONT

Lengthen 1½"

step 3

3. **Add fullness to the outer skirt.** Trace a second copy of both the front and back skirt pattern pieces (with the yokes cut off). Use one set to draft the outer skirt by slashing and spreading the skirt front and back to two times the original width, using the "rocking horse" technique (see pages 167–168). Lengthen both front and back by 1½".

4. **Draft the lining.** Shorten the remaining copy of the front and back pattern pieces by 1½".

5. **Complete the pattern.** Add grainlines and indicate to cut the skirt front, skirt back, and yokes on the fabric fold. Add ½" seam allowance to all the seamlines and along the hemlines. No hem allowances are needed.

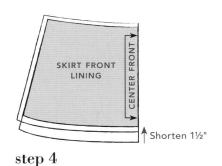

SKIRT FRONT LINING

CENTER FRONT

Shorten 1½"

step 4

PATTERN DRAFTING NOTE

A bubble hem requires an outer skirt and a lining. The hem is created by adding flare and fullness to the outer skirt, and then attaching it at the hemline to the lining, which is shorter and has less flare.

Sew the New Twist Skirt

1. **Cut out the fabric.** Use the newly drafted pattern pieces to cut the following:

   - *From exterior fabric:* one skirt front, one skirt back, two yoke fronts, and two back yokes all on the fabric fold.
   - *From the lining:* one lining front and one lining back on the fabric fold.
   - *From interfacing:* one front and one back yoke on the fold.

2. **Apply interfacing.** Following the manufacturer's instructions, fuse the interfacing to the wrong side of one front and one back yoke.

3. **Assemble the outer skirt.** With the right sides together and raw edges aligned, stitch the back skirts to the front skirt along the side seams, leaving the zipper area open on the left side seam. (The zipper extends through the yoke so the skirt opening is only 4".) Repeat for the lining.

   Run one or two rows of basting stitches along the top edge of both the skirt back and front within the seam allowance (but not the lining); break the stitching in the center front and center back so it is easier to gather the fabric. Only backstitch at one end of the stitching. Repeat to add gathering stitches at the bottom edge of the front and back skirt.

4. **Gather the hemline.** Gently pull the bobbin thread of the basting stitches to gather the hemline until it matches the circumference of the lining hemline.

FABRIC NOTE

The bubble skirt shown here is made with lining fabric for the inside layer to minimize bulk. If your fabric is lightweight, you can use it for both the outside and the inside layer if you prefer.

SUPPLIES

> 2 yards of 44/45" exterior fabric
> 1½ yards of 44/45" lining fabric
> ¾ yard of fusible interfacing
> 7" zipper
> Zipper presser foot
> 4 hook and eye sets
> Matching thread

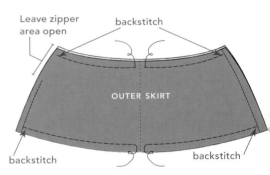

Leave zipper area open

backstitch

OUTER SKIRT

backstitch

backstitch

step 3

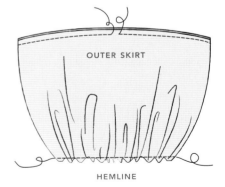

OUTER SKIRT

HEMLINE

step 4

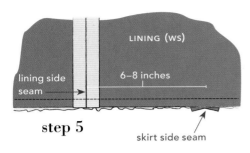

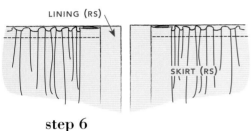

step 5

skirt side seam

step 6

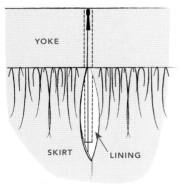

step 9

5. **Attach the two hemlines.** Pin the hemline of the skirt and the hemline of the lining with the right sides together. If you want a twisted hemline, offset the side seams by 6" to 8". Then stitch the seam.

6. **Attach the two top edges.** Press the seam allowance along the zipper opening of the outer skirt to the wrong side and clean finish (pages 33–35) the edges. Turn the skirt so the wrong sides of the lining and skirt are together and repeat step 4 to gather the top edge of the skirt to match the lining. Keep the side seams aligned and pin the top edge of the skirt and lining together. The lining should extend by ½" beyond the outer skirt at the center back.

7. **Assemble the yoke.** With the right sides together and raw edges aligned, stitch the two interfaced back yokes to the interfaced front yoke at the right side seam. Repeat with remaining yoke.

8. **Attach the yoke.** With the right sides together and right side seams aligned, stitch the yoke to the top edge of the skirt. Press the seam allowance toward the yoke.

9. **Install the zipper.** Baste the zipper area closed through the lining and yoke only (don't include the outer skirt in the stitching). Then stitch a centered zipper (page 40) in the yoke and lining seam. Align the top zipper stop with the seamline at the top edge of the skirt. Leave the outer skirt free.

10. **Finish the yoke.** Press the left side and bottom seam allowances of the yoke facing ½" to the wrong side. With the right sides together, stitch the yoke facing to the yoke at the top edge. Press the seam allowances toward the yoke facing and understitch. Turn the facing to the wrong side and hand-sew the left side edges of the facing to the zipper tape and the bottom edge to cover the seam allowance.

11. **Add a hook and eye** at the top of the zipper opening inside the skirt. To keep the outer skirt closed while wearing, sew the remaining hooks and eyes inside the zipper opening of the outer skirt.

SATURDAY

Violet Femme Skirt

Design Variation: Faced Pleats

This skirt has tailored elegance, but the peek-a-boo option of contrasting pleat facings makes it suitable for much more than business. Faced pleats require an extra pattern piece for the interior of each pleat. The extra piece adds more flare when the skirt is in motion, but typically falls behind the pleat folds when the wearer is standing still. This detail also works as a beautiful substitution for a kick pleat in a straight skirt.

Make the pleat(s) as deep as you like, by drafting the pleat facing or extension to the desired depth. This skirt does not have pleats in the back, but you can add them if you would like.

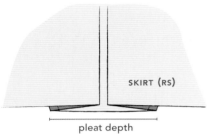

step 4a

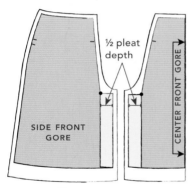

step 4b

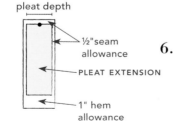

step 5

Draft the Pattern

1. **Trace your basic flared front and back skirt patterns** (page 163) onto drafting paper. Do not add any seam or hem allowances yet, but do trace any darts. Lower the waistline (page 65) and lengthen or shorten the skirt (page 70) as desired.

2. **Draft a traditional, one-piece waistband pattern** with a separate facing and a left side seam extension, following the instructions on pages 65–66. Add ½" seam allowance around the edges.

3. **Add gores to your skirt** following the instructions on pages 177–178, turning the skirt into a six-gore design. Trace the four gore pattern pieces without any seam allowance. The center front and center back will be cut on the fabric fold and the zipper will be in the left side seam.

4. **Plan the pleats. a)** Decide how deep you would like each pleat to be.

   b) Draft a pleat extension on the seamlines that join the front and side front gore pieces. Each pleat extension should be as wide as half the desired pleat depth and as long as the desired length of the pleat opening. The pleats in this skirt are 5" deep and 13¾" long. Add ½" seam allowance to all the gore pieces and add 1" hem allowance. Add a registration dot at the top of each extension.

5. **Draft the pleat facing** to be as wide as the desired pleat depth and as long as the desired pleat length. Add a registration dot at the top center. Add ½" seam allowance around the side and top edges and 1" hem allowance along the bottom edge.

6. **Complete the pattern.** Add grainlines to the patterns indicating to cut the center front and center back on the fabric fold. Add ½" seam allowances to all of the gore pieces. Add 1" hem allowance. Plan for an invisible (or regular) zipper at the left side seam.

Sew the Skirt

1. **Cut out the fabric.** Use the newly drafted pattern pieces to cut the following:

   - *From fabric:* one skirt center front and one skirt center back on the fabric fold, two side fronts and two side backs, two waistbands, and two pleat facings (one for each pleat).

   - *From interfacing:* one waistband.

2. **Apply interfacing.** Following the manufacturer's instructions, fuse the interfacing to the wrong side of one waistband.

3. **Assemble the skirt front. a)** With the right sides together, stitch the side front panels to the center front panel, from the top edge to the registration dot at the beginning of the extension; backstitch.

   b) Press open the skirt seam allowance above the pleat opening. Pin a facing to the seam allowances of the pleat opening with the right sides together, matching the dots and aligning the raw edges. Stitch one long edge of the facing, from the hem up, and then pivot to stitch across the top edge to the seam, ending the stitching at the dot; backstitch. Repeat to stitch the other side of the facing. Repeat for the remaining pleat.

4. **Assemble the skirt back.** With the right sides together and raw edges aligned, stitch the side back panels to the center-back panel.

5. **Sew the side seams.** Stitch the front to the back at the *right* side seam. Install the invisible zipper in the *left* side seam as on page 41.

6. **Assemble and attach the waistband,** per the one-piece waistband pattern with a separate facing and a side seam extension as on pages 65–66.

7. **Hem the skirt.** Carefully press under a ½" double-fold hem. Hand-stitch close to the inner folded edge, or sew the hem as desired (pages 45–51).

SUPPLIES

> 2 yards of 44/45" fabric
> ¼ yard of fusible interfacing
> 7" invisible zipper
> Invisible zipper presser foot
> Hook and eye
> Matching thread

SKIRT (WS)

step 3a

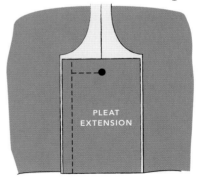

PLEAT EXTENSION

step 3b

chapter 7 / HIGH−WAISTED SKIRTS

For a look that's both classic and modern, try a high-waisted skirt. If you thought these looks were only suited for vintage costumes, think again. Paired with a chic blouse and cute shoes, they're surprisingly flattering on many different body types.

The process of drafting a high waist is super simple with an end result that looks tailored and polished. The next seven projects start with the basic high-waist pattern and change it up with plenty of different hem and waistline options. If you can draw a straight line with a ruler, you can master these looks in no time.

High-Waisted Skirt

Draft the Basic Pattern

For many people, a skirt that sits on the natural waist is already high, especially after wearing low-waisted styles. However, for those of you that love retro or more feminine looks, the high-waisted silhouette is a fun option. The waistline is raised above the natural line, often creating the illusion of a smaller waist.

Draft the Pattern

1. **Trace your basic, customized skirt front sloper** onto drafting paper. Do not include seam or hem allowance but do trace the darts. Make the following adjustments:

   - Raise the waistline as much as you like (typically 2" to 2½") by drawing in a new waistline, parallel to the existing seamline.

   - Shave ¼" off the side seam, starting at the top edge of the new waistline and tapering to nothing at the old waistline, to make the skirt slightly more close-fitted.

   - Mark registration dots at the original waistline on each dart. Extend the dart legs straight up from the registration dots to the new waistline.

2. **Repeat for the skirt back,** raising the waistline to match the front.

3. **Draft a facing pattern** as explained on page 70.

4. **Complete the pattern.** Add ½" seam allowances to all the pattern edges, except the center front and back, which should be cut on the fabric fold. There is a zipper in the center-back seam. Add 1½" hem allowance, or as desired.

step 1

PATTERN DRAFTING NOTE

Once you draft your basic high-waisted patterns, before adding seam and hem allowances, copy them onto patternmaking or drafting paper so you can use them as the starting point for several of the high-waisted skirts in this chapter.

Sew the Basic High-Waisted Skirt

SUPPLIES

> 1½ yards of 44/45" fabric
> 1 yard of fusible interfacing
> 7" zipper
> Zipper presser foot
> Hook and eye
> Matching thread

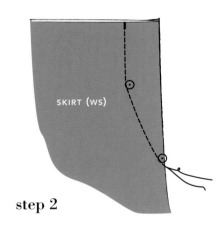

step 2

1. **Cut out the fabric.** Use the newly drafted pattern pieces to cut the following:

   - *From fabric:* one skirt front on the fabric fold, two skirt backs, one front facing on the fabric fold, and two back facings.

   - *From interfacing:* one front facing on the fold and two back facings.

2. **Apply interfacing.** Following the manufacturer's instructions, fuse the interfacing to the wrong side of each facing piece.

3. **Stitch the darts.** When you pin the darts, make sure the waistline registration dots are aligned. Machine-stitch from the top edge to the registration points, make a soft turn, and continue on to the dart point. Press the darts flat toward the center front.

4. **Install a lapped zipper** in the center-back seam (see pages 42–43).

5. **Sew the side seams.** With right sides together, stitch the skirt front and skirt back at the side seams.

6. **For how to add a facing,** see page 70.

7. **Hem the skirt.** Press under the bottom edge ½" to the wrong side, then press under another 1". Machine-stitch or hand-sew the hem as desired (see pages 45–51).

SUNDAY

Jazz Age Skirt

Design Variation: Trumpet Silhouette

A trumpet-shaped skirt is fitted through the hips and flares at the hem. You can add a little flare or a lot. You can also start the flare as high as you like on the body. A stiff fabric will hold the shape dramatically, while lighter weight fabric will cascade down, much like a flounce.

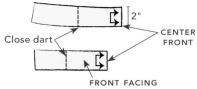

Close dart — FRONT FACING — CENTER FRONT — 2"

step 2

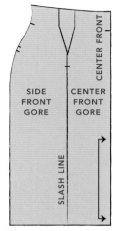

CENTER FRONT

SIDE FRONT GORE — CENTER FRONT GORE

SLASH LINE

step 3

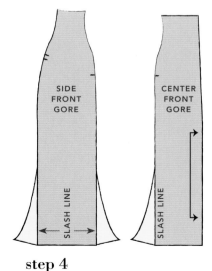

SIDE FRONT GORE — CENTER FRONT GORE

SLASH LINE — SLASH LINE

step 4

Draft the Pattern

1. **Trace your high-waisted patterns** (page 199) onto drafting paper, leaving space all around for design features. Make sure the pattern you start with does not have any seam or hem allowances included yet. Change the pattern into a one-dart pattern (see page 64).

2. **Draft the front and back waistline facings.** Draft a 2"-wide facing down the skirt front and back slopers. Onto drafting paper, trace the facings from both patterns (trace the top edge of the skirt, the center and side edges for 2", and the facing design line). Tape the darts closed. Add ½" seam allowances to all the edges except the center front and center back, which should be cut on the fabric fold.

3. **Divide the front and back skirt patterns** to make a six-gore silhouette. Start by drawing a line from the dart point straight down to the hemline, parallel to the center front. Repeat for the skirt back.

   Cut the front and back patterns apart along the line. Smooth the dart edges to eliminate any hard corners at the waist seamline. It helps to label the pieces as follows: center front, side front, center back, side back. Make note to cut two of all the skirt pieces, except the center front, which will be cut on the fabric fold. Plan for a center-back zipper, so do not cut the center-back gore on the fabric fold.

4. **Decide how much flare** you want to add to the hemline and where on the skirt you want the flare to begin (at hipline, knees, or high hip). Extend the seams of each gore out at the hemline. Blend the extension from the hemline to the desired starting point of the flare using a curved ruler. Do not add flare to the center-back seam.

5. **Complete the pattern.** Add grainlines and registration marks to all of your pattern pieces. Add ½" seam allowances. If you are going to sew horsehair in the hem, add hem allowance at least ½" wider than the braid; otherwise, add ½" hem allowance.

Sew the Jazz Age Skirt

1. **Cut out the fabric.** Use the newly drafted pattern pieces to cut the following:

   - *From fabric:* one center-front gore and one front facing on the fabric fold, two side-front gores, two side-back gores, two center-back gores, and two back facings.

   - *From interfacing:* one front facing on the fold and two back facings.

2. **Apply interfacing.** Following the manufacturer's instructions, fuse the interfacing to the wrong side of the facings.

3. **Assemble the front.** With the right sides together and raw edges aligned, stitch the center-front gore to the side-front gores. Press the seam allowances open.

4. **Install an invisible zipper** (page 41) in the center-back seam. With the right sides together and raw edges aligned, stitch the back gore to the side-back gores. Press the seam allowances open.

5. **Sew the side seams.** With the right sides together and raw edges aligned, stitch the skirt back to the skirt front at the side seams and press the seam allowances open.

DESIGN NOTE

Consider using an invisible zipper for this skirt. It blends right in, looks just like a seam, and is simple to sew. You can also make this skirt look very different depending on the amount of flare you add at the hem and how high up on the skirt you begin the flare. This skirt alone can have several different looks.

SUPPLIES

> 2⅞ yards of 44/45" fabric
> ¾ yard of fusible interfacing
> 11" invisible zipper
> Invisible zipper presser foot
> Hook and eye
> Matching thread
> ½"-wide horsehair braid (optional)

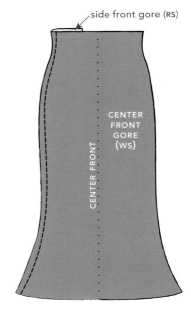

side front gore (RS)

CENTER FRONT GORE (WS)

CENTER FRONT

step 3

6. **Assemble the facing.** With right sides together and raw edges aligned, stitch the two back facings to the center-front facing at the side seams. Press the seam allowances open. Press the bottom and center-back edges of the facing ½" to the wrong side. Edgestitch the bottom edge for a clean finish.

7. **Attach the facing.** With the right sides together and top edges aligned, pin the facing to the skirt. Make sure the side seams are aligned and that the pressed back edges of the facing align with the center-back opening. Stitch.

   Press the seam allowance toward the facing and understitch. Hand-sew the facing edges in place along the zipper opening and hand-tack it at each side seam. See Piece Gathering Skirt on page 188, step 7 for more information.

8. **Hem the skirt** as desired. Or, as for the skirt shown here, insert horsehair braid in the hem (page 51) to stiffen it and exaggerate the trumpet silhouette.

Coney Island Skirt

Design Variation: Sailor-Style Front Opening

For a skirt that looks great on the boardwalk and the catwalk, try this nautical style complete with contrast stitching. Featuring a functional button closure inspired by sailor trousers, this skirt is sure to be a summertime favorite. Use topstitching thread in a contrasting color for the most visible stitching on the skirt and to highlight the nautical theme.

MONDAY

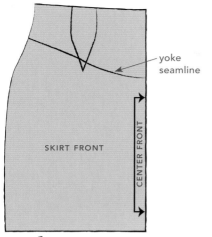

step 1

SKIRT FRONT

CENTER FRONT

yoke seamline

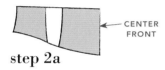

step 2a

CENTER FRONT

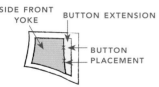

step 2b

SIDE FRONT YOKE

BUTTON EXTENSION

BUTTON PLACEMENT

BUTTON EXTENSION

CENTER FRONT YOKE

BUTTONHOLE PLACEMENT

CENTER FRONT

Draft the Pattern

1. **Trace your high-waisted skirt front and back slopers** (page 199) onto drafting paper, leaving space all around for design features and seam allowances. Change the design to a one-dart silhouette (page 64). Draw the yoke seamline on the skirt front so it falls just above or below the dart point. Make it as deep and as shaped as you wish. Cut off the yoke.

2. **Draft the yoke pattern pieces. a)** This skirt has button closures *in the location of the darts,* so cut the yoke apart along the dart legs and discard the inside of the darts. Label the side piece as side-front yoke. Label the center piece as the center-front yoke and indicate for it to be cut on the fabric fold.

   b) To the dart side of each yoke piece, add a button extension that is as wide as twice the diameter of the button. Add ½" seam allowance around all the edges, except for the center front (it is cut on the fold). Mark the placement of buttons and buttonholes (refer to the photograph on page 205).

3. **Add a cluster of gathers in the front. a)** Below the yoke seam, measure what is left of any remaining dart and shave it off the side seam (if your yoke design line was below the point of the dart, disregard). Then draw a slash line from the side seam to the desired location for the center of the gathers.

   b) Tape the center front of the skirt pattern onto drafting paper, slash the line from the yoke seamline to (but not through) the side seam. Spread the side section about 4" to create extra room for the gathers shown. Smooth out the yoke seam. It will be easier to cut the fabric if you trace the slashed-and-spread pattern to create a new, neater skirt front pattern.

TIP The shape of the back yoke can be different, and often not as deep, as the front yoke as long as it aligns at the side seams.

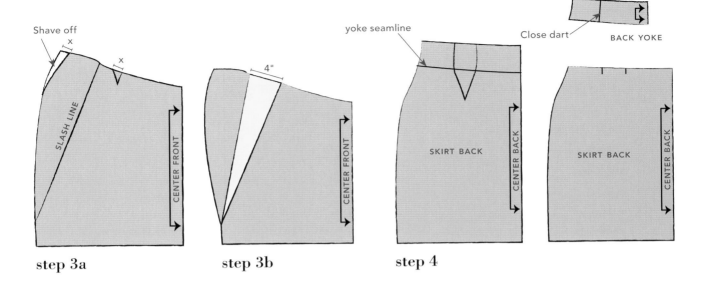

step 3a   step 3b   step 4

4. **Draw the yoke seamline on the skirt back,** aligning it with the skirt front at the side seam. Cut off the yoke and close the dart in the yoke to create the yoke pattern. You can leave any remaining dart below the yoke and sew it into a dart during construction, or mark to become a pleat as shown. The original dart legs become the pleat markings.

5. **Complete the pattern.** Add grainlines and registration marks to all of the pattern pieces. Add ½" seam allowances to all seam edges except those cut on the fabric fold and add 2" hem allowance.

PATTERN DRAFTING NOTE

The skirt front yoke is made from three panels so the buttons are functional. However, you can simply make it from one piece and topstitch the details for a trompe l'oeil effect. Because of the hourglass shape, you'll still need a zipper to get in and out of the skirt.

> 2¼ yards of 44/45" fabric
> 1 yard of fusible interfacing
> 11" zipper (invisible or regular)
> Zipper presser foot
> Hook and eye
> 4 buttons
> Topstitching thread
> Topstitching machine needle (optional)
> Matching thread

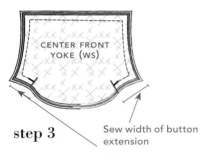

step 3

Sew width of button extension

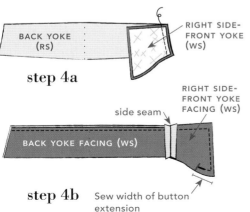

step 4a

step 4b Sew width of button extension

Sew the Coney Island Skirt

1. **Cut out the fabric.** Use the newly drafted pattern pieces to cut the following:

   - *From fabric:* one skirt front and one skirt back on the fabric fold, two center-front yokes and two center-back yokes on the fabric fold, four side-front yokes.

   - *From interfacing:* one center-front yoke and one center-back yoke on the fold and two side-front yokes.

2. **Apply interfacing.** Following the manufacturer's instructions, fuse the interfacing to the wrong side of one center-front yoke, one center-back yoke, and two side-front yokes.

3. **Assemble the center-front yoke.** With the right sides together and raw edges aligned, stitch the two center-front yokes together around the side and top edges. Stitch the bottom edges only along the button extensions on each side, as shown; backstitch. Then, snip with scissors into the seam allowance at the backstitches, through all the layers. Trim the corners and turn the yoke right side out.

4. **Assemble the right side-front and back yoke.** a) With the right sides together and edges aligned, stitch the interfaced right side-front yoke to the interfaced back yoke at the side seam as shown. Press the seam allowance open. Repeat with the remaining (non-interfaced) right side-front yoke and back yoke to make the facing for this piece.

   b) With the right sides together and raw edges aligned, stitch these two assembled pieces together around the top and front side edges as shown. Pivot at the bottom of the right front side edge and stitch along the bottom edge for the length of the button extension only; backstitch. Leave the left side seam open. Then, snip into the seam allowance at the backstitches, through all the layers. Trim the corners and turn the yoke right side out.

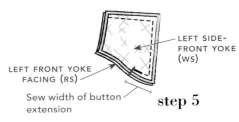

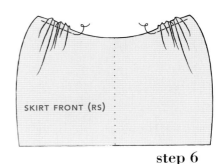

step 5

5. **Assemble the left side-front yoke.** With the right sides together, stitch the two remaining yoke pieces together along the top and front edges. Pivot at the bottom of the front edge and stitch along the bottom edge for the length of the button extension only; backstitch. Leave the left side seam open. Then, snip into the seam allowance at the backstitches, through all the layers. Trim the corners and turn the yoke right side out.

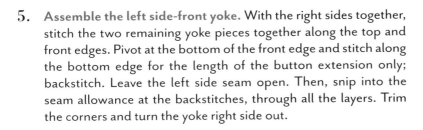

6. **Gather the skirt front.** Run one or two rows of basting stitches along the two areas to be gathered. Pull the bobbin threads to gather the skirt to fit the yokes. Don't knot the threads yet, just in case you have to adjust the gathering to fit the yoke when you attach it.

step 6

7. **Stitch the back darts** or stitch the pleats depending on how you drafted the skirt back.

8. **Sew the right side seam.** With the right sides together and right side seams aligned, stitch the skirt front to the skirt back along the right side seam. The left side seam has an invisible zipper and will be stitched later.

9. **Attach the yoke pieces to the skirt. a)** With the right sides together and side seams aligned, stitch the yoke piece from step 4 to the back and right front side of the skirt. Align the center backs and side seams. Fold the facing seam allowance out of the way so the seam is easier to sew. Be careful to not sew through the facing. Press the seam allowance toward the yoke. Repeat to stitch the left side-front yoke to the left side of the skirt front.

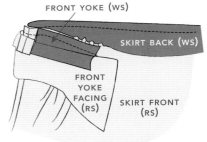

step 9a

   b) With the right sides together and raw edges aligned, center the front yoke on the skirt front and fold the facing seam allowance out of the way to make it easier to sew. The raw edges should align with the side-front yokes, with the button extensions overlapping. Stitch the center-front yoke to the skirt front, being careful to not sew through the facing. Press the seam allowance toward the yoke.

10. **Insert an invisible or regular zipper** in the left side seam through the skirt and yoke pieces (pages 40–43).

11. **Finish the yokes.** Press the bottom and left side seam allowances of the yoke facings ½" to the wrong side and fold them so they cover and encase all the raw edges. Stitch in the ditch (tip on page 69) at the yoke seamline. Hand-sew the side edges to the zipper tape.

12. **Make the buttonholes.** Try on the skirt and check the best location for the four horizontal buttonholes on the front yoke. See pages 38–39 for buttonhole information, and refer to your sewing machine manual for how to machine-stitch buttonholes. Hand-sew the buttons in place.

13. **Hem the skirt.** Press the hem edge ½" to the wrong side and then 1½" again. Topstitch with contrast thread (install a topstitching needle) along the inner pressed edge. Or hem the skirt using your preferred method (pages 45–51).

TUESDAY

French Toast Skirt

Design Variation: Gored Pockets

This skirt, made in cashmere and wool, looks very elegant — however, it looks just as great made from a casual fabric like chambray. The V-shaped details add unexpected style to the simple silhouette, while the expanded pockets give you a place to store things you need close at hand.

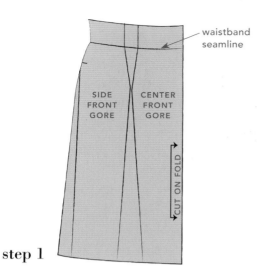

waistband seamline

SIDE FRONT GORE

CENTER FRONT GORE

CUT ON FOLD

step 1

Draft the Pattern

1. **Trace your basic flared skirt front and back patterns** (page 163) onto drafting paper. Do not add any seam or hem allowances, but do trace the darts. Draft a high waist following the instructions on page 199 and draw a 2"-wide waistband seamline. Draft the skirt into a six-gore silhouette (pages 177–178), but don't cut the gores apart yet.

2. **Draft the waistband.** Cut off the front and back waistbands and tape the darts closed to create a contoured waistband (page 67). Draw a V-shaped dip at the center of the top edge of the front waistband. Plan for a zipper in the left side seam.

3. **Mark the gore panels.** Trace the front, back, side-front, and side-back gore panels onto drafting paper as on page 178. Include registration marks (page 72). Remember you can't cut the gores apart because you added shape to the seamlines.

4. **Plot the pocket** on the side-front gore, by simply drawing the top and bottom at the desired location. This pocket is 6½" long by the width of the gore panel.

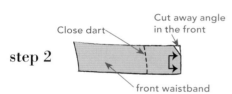

Cut away angle in the front

Close dart

step 2

front waistband

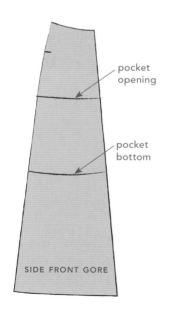

pocket opening

pocket bottom

SIDE FRONT GORE

step 4

PATTERN DRAFTING NOTE

The pockets on this pattern are drafted to stand out from the skirt slightly. If you don't like this detail, simply omit the slash-and-spread technique from step 5. To make the pocket, you need three pattern pieces: side-front gore backing, side-front gore, and pocket lining. They are drafted from the side-front gore (which is not used as a whole piece to make the skirt).

5. **Widen the pocket. a)** On a separate piece of drafting paper, trace the side-front gore from the hemline up to the pocket opening. Draw a vertical slash line through the center, from the top pocket opening to the bottom of the pocket.

   b) Spread the opening so the pocket flares slightly. To do this, cut the slash line from the pocket opening to the bottom edge of the pocket. Spread the pieces about 2". Tape the spread pieces to pattern drafting paper and add a V-shaped detail at the center of the top edge of the pocket. This becomes the side-front gore pattern.

6. **For the side-front gore backing** pattern piece, trace the side-front gore (from step 3) from the top/waistline edge to the bottom of the pocket onto drafting paper.

7. **For the pocket lining** pattern piece, trace the side-front gore (from step 5) from the top of the pocket to the bottom of the pocket onto drafting paper.

8. **Complete the pattern.** Add grainlines (cut the center-front gore on the fabric fold) and registration marks to all of your pattern pieces. Add ½" seam allowance for all the seam edges including the shaped waistband and pockets. Add 2" hem allowance.

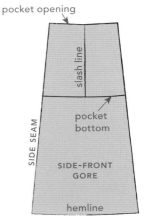

step 5a

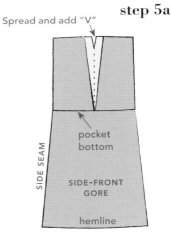

step 5b

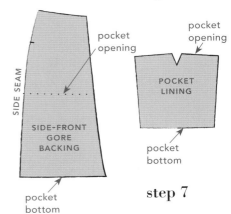

step 7

> 2½ yards of 44/45" fabric
> ¾ yard of fusible interfacing
> ¼ yard of lining for pockets
> 11" zipper
> Zipper presser foot
> Hook and eye
> Matching thread

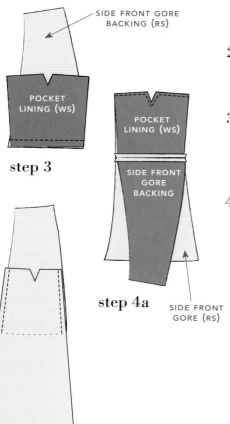

step 3

step 4a

step 4b

Sew the French Toast Skirt

1. **Cut out the fabric.** Use the newly drafted pattern pieces to cut the following:

   - *From fabric, on the fold:* one skirt front/gore, one skirt back/gore, two front waistbands, and two back waistbands
   - *From fabric, also cut:* two side-front gores, two side-front gore backings, and two side-back gores.
   - *From lining:* two pocket linings.
   - *From interfacing:* one front and one back waistband on the fold.

2. **Apply interfacing.** Following the manufacturer's instructions, fuse the interfacing to the wrong side of one front waistband and one back waistband.

3. **Attach the pocket lining** to the side-front gore backing with the right sides and bottom edges together. Stitch along the bottom edge. Repeat for the remaining pocket lining and side-front backing.

4. **Attach pocket linings to side-front gores. a)** With the right sides together and top edges aligned, stitch each pocket lining to its coordinating side-front gore piece along the top edge. Trim the seam allowances of the V opening and turn the pocket right side out. Repeat for the remaining pocket lining and side-front gore. If you want to topstitch the top edge of the pocket openings, do so now.

   b) Pin the side edges of the side-front gore backing, pocket lining, and side-front gore together. This will cause the pocket to stand away from the pocket backing (as designed). Baste the side edges together. Repeat with the remaining side-front gore backing, pocket lining, pocket backing, and side-front gore pieces.

5. **Assemble the skirt front.** With the right sides together and raw edges aligned, stitch one side-front gore (with pocket) to each side of the center-front gore. Press the seams open.

6. **Assemble the skirt back.** With the right sides together and raw edges aligned, stitch one side-back gore to each side of the center-back gore. Press the seams open.

7. **Sew the side seams.** Join the skirt front and back at the right side seam and install a lapped or invisible zipper (pages 41–43) in the left side seam.

8. **Assemble the waistband and waistband facing.** With the right sides together and side seams aligned, stitch the interfaced back waistband to the interfaced front waistband at the right side seam. Press the seam allowances open. Repeat with the remaining waistband pieces to make the waistband facing.

9. **Attach the waistband.** With the right sides together and raw edges aligned, stitch the assembled waistband to the skirt, making sure the right side seams are together. The waistband seam allowances should extend beyond the zipper opening in the left side seam (see how to sew a waistband extension on pages 68–69).

10. **Attach the waistband facing.** With the right sides together and raw edges aligned, stitch the waistband facing to the waistband along the top edge; make sure to pivot at the V-opening. Trim the seam allowances of the V-opening and trim the corners. Turn the waistband to the inside of the skirt and press. Turn under the remaining raw edges of the waistband facing along the bottom and zipper edges. Hand-sew the turned edges in place along the zipper and opening. You can add three rows of topstitching, ¼" apart, to the finished waistband as desired (see photo on this page).

11. **Hem the skirt.** Press under the hem edge ½" to the wrong side, then another 1½". Topstitch along the inner pressed edge. Or hem the skirt using your preferred method (pages 45–51).

WAISTBAND FACING (WS)

SKIRT FRONT (RS)

step 10

Happy Hour Skirt

Design Variation: Button Tab Closure

This skirt uses a button tab to cinch in the waist, creating an hourglass silhouette. It flatters many body types, giving curves to those with straighter shaped bodies and creating a smaller waistline for full-figured ladies. The inverted box pleats at the waistline are not stitched in place; instead, by buttoning the tab and closing the snaps, the pleats are held closed and the skirt is easy to take on and off. The button tab is held in place with both buttons and snaps.

Draft the Pattern

1. **Trace your basic flared skirt front and back patterns** (page 163) onto drafting paper. Do not add any seam or hem allowances, but do trace any darts. Draft a high waist following the instructions on page 199. Add a slash line extending from the dart point to the hemline on both the skirt front and back.

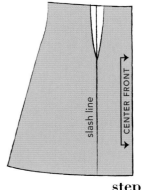

step 1

2. **Decide how deep you want each pleat** (page 182). (The pleats on this skirt are 2½" deep.) Then slash the pattern from the waist edge, along one dart leg to the hemline and spread it twice the desired depth. Tape the spread pattern onto drafting paper.

3. **Mark the pleat foldlines** as shown. Repeat for the skirt back.

4. **Draft the pleat tab.** Fold the pattern paper as you would the pleat. Then, using a separate piece of paper, draw the tab pattern (refer to illustration on the next page).

    *   Center the paper over the natural waistline (and folded pleat), extending from the center front (as shown). Make sure the tab pattern extends from the center front past the underlying pleat layers.

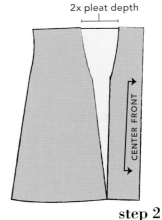

step 2

    *   Measure the diameter of your button and make sure the tab is long and wide enough to accommodate your button. (The tab on this skirt is 2" wide.) Mark the button placement on the tab so it is about ¾" away from the outside edge (marked with the left X on the illustration). Mark the same button placement on the skirt pattern.

    *   Repeat to draft the tab for the skirt back.

    *   Add ½" seam allowance around the tabs except for the center front and center back, which are cut on the fabric fold.

step 3

    *   Draw the buttonhole centered on the tab, starting ⅛" outside the button placement. (For help determining the correct buttonhole length, see page 38.)

    *   Add a placement marking for the snap just to the right of the pleat foldline closest to the center front on both the skirt pattern and the tab.

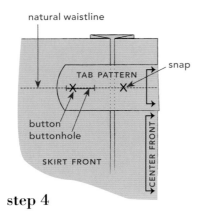

natural waistline

TAB PATTERN

snap

button
buttonhole

CENTER FRONT

SKIRT FRONT

step 4

SUPPLIES

> 2 yards of 44/45" fabric
> ¾ yard of fusible interfacing
> 4 snaps
> 4 buttons, about 1¼" diameter
> Matching thread

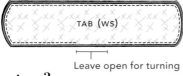

TAB (WS)

Leave open for turning

step 3

5. **Draft the facing pattern pieces.** Unfold the pleat and trace the top edge of the skirt front. Draw a line 4" from and parallel to the top edge to mark the bottom edge of the facing. Trace the entire facing on separate paper. Repeat for the skirt back.

6. **Complete the pattern.** Add grainlines and registration marks to all of your pattern pieces. Add ½" seam allowance for all the seams. Add 2" for the hem allowance.

Sew the Happy Hour Skirt

1. **Cut out the fabric.** Use the newly drafted pattern pieces to cut the following:

   • *From fabric, all on the fold:* one skirt front, one front facing, and one front tab; one skirt back, one back facing, and one back tab. If desired, transfer the foldline markings onto the fabric.

   • *From interfacing, on the fold:* one front and one back facing, and one front and one back tab.

2. **Apply interfacing.** Following the manufacturer's instructions, fuse the interfacing to the wrong side of the facings and the tabs.

3. **Stitch the tabs.** With right sides together, stitch the two front tabs, leaving an opening for turning. Clip/trim seam allowance and turn the tab right side out. Turn the raw edges at the opening to the inside and press. Edgestitch around all the edges of the tab. Repeat with the back tab pieces.

4. **Stitch buttonholes.** Referring to your pattern for placement and your sewing machine manual for instructions, stitch two buttonholes on each button tab. Make sure they are centered.

5. **Assemble the skirt.** With the right sides together, stitch the skirt front to the skirt back at the side seams. Press the seam allowances open.

6. **Assemble the facing.** With the right sides together, stitch the front facing to the back facing at the side seams. Press the seam allowances open. Press the bottom edge seam allowance to the wrong side and topstitch it in place to finish the edges.

7. **Attach the facing.** With the right sides together and raw edges aligned, stitch the facing to the top edge of the skirt. Make sure the side seams are aligned. Press the seam allowance toward the facing and understitch (page 37). Hand-tack the facings down at the side seams.

8. **Press the pleats and add the tab.** Refer to the marked foldlines to press the pleats into the skirt front and back and pin them in place (do not stitch them closed). Position the button tab over the skirt front and mark the placement on the skirt for the buttons and snaps. Repeat for the skirt back. Unpin the tabs.

9. **Hand-sew the buttons** and snaps at the marked locations on the skirt. Sew the coordinating snap pieces on the tabs. Button and snap the tabs in place; unbutton and unsnap to get in and out of the skirt.

10. **Hem the skirt.** Carefully press under the lower edge of the skirt ½" to the wrong side, then another 1½". Hand-sew close to the inner folded edge, or sew the hem as desired (pages 45–51).

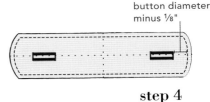

button diameter minus ⅛"

step 4

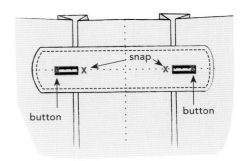

snap

button   button

step 8

TIP You can spray starch the pleats if you want to make them even more defined.

THURSDAY

Nip and Tuck Skirt

Design Variation: Release Tucks

Tucked pleats, also called released tucks, are a combination of a tuck and a pleat. However, unlike the tucks shown on page 108, these are sewn with the right sides together. They also only add fullness to the waistline, leaving the hemline to swing unchanged.

Draft the Pattern

1. **Trace your basic flared skirt front and back patterns** (page 163) onto drafting paper. Make the following adjustments:

   - Do not add any seam or hem allowances yet, but do trace the darts. The front has a center zipper, but the center back can be cut on the fabric fold.

   - For both front and back slopers, draft a high waist following the instructions on page 199.

   - Draft a contoured waistband with a center front opening (page 67).

   - For the front sloper only, add a slash line extending from the dart point to the hemline. (The back of the skirt has a normal dart.) Cut out and discard the dart.

2. **Slash the dart open** along both dart legs and then down the slash line to the hem. Don't cut through the hemline. Spread the pattern by your desired tuck amount (this skirt was spread about 1½").

3. **Draft the tucks.** Draw stitching lines for the tucks along the original dart legs. Measure from the top edge to the desired tuck length (the tuck for this skirt was 7" long). At that point draw a horizontal line from dart leg to dart leg, as shown. Add ½" seam allowance at all the seams, including the edges of the tuck.

4. **Complete the pattern.** Add grainlines and registration marks to all of the pattern pieces and 2" hem allowance.

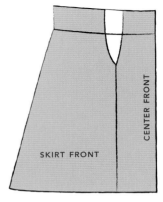

step 1

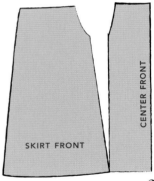

step 2

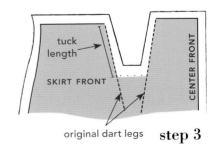

step 3

Sew the Nip and Tuck Skirt

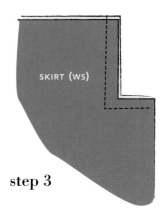

SKIRT (WS)

step 3

1. **Cut out the fabric.** Use the newly drafted pattern pieces to cut the following:

   - *From fabric:* two skirt fronts and four front waistbands; one skirt back and two back waistbands on the fabric fold.

   - *From interfacing:* one back waistband on the fold and two front waistbands.

2. **Apply interfacing.** Following the manufacturer's instructions, fuse the interfacing to the wrong side of two front waistbands and one back waistband.

3. **Stitch the front tucks.** With the right sides together and raw edges aligned, stitch each tuck closed. Stitch from the top edge and pivot across the bottom of each tuck; backstitch or knot the threads. Then press each tuck toward the side seam.

4. **Stitch the back darts** (page 35).

5. **Sew the side seams.** With the right sides together and edges aligned, stitch the skirt fronts to the back at the side seams. Press the seam allowances open.

6. **Assemble the waistband and waistband facing.** With the right sides together and edges aligned, stitch the two front interfaced waistbands to the back interfaced waistband at the side seams. Press the seam allowances open. Repeat with the remaining waistband pieces to make the waistband facing. Press the bottom and center front seam allowances of the facing to the wrong side.

CONSTRUCTION NOTE
Sew the tucks before joining the skirt front and back together at the side seams.

7. **Attach the waistband.** With the right sides together and top edges aligned, stitch the assembled waistband to the skirt. Make sure the side seams are aligned and the center front edges meet. Press the seam allowance toward the waistband and understitch (page 37).

8. **Install an exposed zipper** to the center-front seam (page 44). Finish the remainder of the seam.

9. **Attach the waistband facing.** With the right sides together and raw edges aligned, stitch the waistband facing to the waistband at the top edge. Fold the facing inside the skirt and hand-sew the center front facing edges in place along the zipper opening. Sew the bottom edge to cover the waistband seam.

10. **Hem the skirt.** Press under the bottom of the skirt ½" to the wrong side, then another 1½". Hand-sew close to the inner folded edge, or sew the hem as desired (pages 45–51).

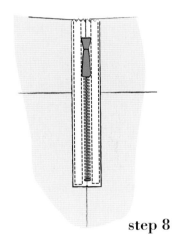

step 8

Hit the Sack Skirt

Design Variation: Paper-Bag Waistline and Sash

Design a paper-bag-waist skirt by drafting a wide pattern at the waist and using pleats at the waist to cinch it in. The skirt shown here is drafted much like the Great Scot Skirt on pages 130–131; however, the top edge is finished with a facing instead of a waistband.

FRIDAY

Draft the Pattern

1. **Trace your basic high-waisted skirt front and back patterns** (page 199) onto drafting paper. Do not add any seam or hem allowances yet. Change the design to a one-dart silhouette (page 64). Draw three evenly spaced slash lines parallel to the center front, positioning one slash line along the dart leg. For more exact plotting instructions, see pleating for the Great Scot Skirt, pages 130–131.

2. **Draft the pleats.** Decide how deep you want each pleat to be (see page 131), and then double that amount. (The pleats in this skirt are about 1½" deep; the doubled measurement would be 3".) Slash and spread the pattern by the doubled amount to create each pleat, and tape the spread pieces onto drafting paper. Mark the original waistline on the pattern.

   Repeat for the skirt back, positioning the pleats in the same way, but allowing for a center-back zipper.

3. **Draft the facing pattern pieces.** Fold the pleats and trace the top edge of the skirt front. Draw a line 4" from and parallel to the top edge to mark the bottom of the facing pattern. Trace the facing pattern onto separate paper. Repeat for the skirt back (with a center-back opening).

4. **Draft a sash.** Draw a rectangle 3" wide by the desired length (the sash for this skirt is 68" long). The sash shown here has angled ends.

5. **Add in-seam pockets.** Follow the instructions on page 93 to draft in-seam pocket patterns that start at the waistline and extend down as deep as you want.

6. **Complete the pattern.** Add grainlines (cut the skirt front and facing on the fabric fold) and registration marks to all of your pattern pieces. Add ½" seam allowances to all the seams and add a 1½" hem allowance.

step 1

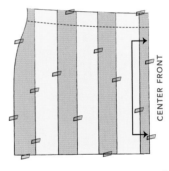

step 2

step 3

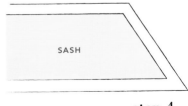

step 4

Sew the Hit the Sack Skirt

SUPPLIES

> 2 yards of 44/45" fabric

> ¾ yard of fusible interfacing

> 11" invisible (or regular) zipper

> Invisible zipper presser foot

> Hook and eye

> 4 buttons

> Matching thread

1. **Cut out the fabric.** Use the newly drafted pattern pieces to cut the following:

   - *From fabric:* one skirt front and one front facing on the fabric fold, two skirt backs, two back facings, four pockets, and two sashes. Transfer all the pleat fold markings from the pattern to the fabric (page 26).

   - *From interfacing:* one front facing on the fold and two back facings.

2. **Apply interfacing.** Following the manufacturer's instructions, fuse the interfacing to the wrong side of the facings.

3. **Install an invisible zipper** in the center-back seam, joining the two back pieces together (page 41).

4. **Sew the pockets and side seams.** Follow the instructions on page 94, steps 4 and 5, to attach the pockets to the skirt front and sew the side seams.

5. **Assemble the facing.** With the right sides together and side seams aligned, stitch the two skirt back facings to the skirt front facing. Press the seam allowances open. Press the bottom edge and center-back seam allowances to the wrong side ½". Topstitch along the bottom edge.

CONSTRUCTION NOTE

Because these pleats are partially stitched down, this skirt requires a zipper to get it on and off. However, if you don't stitch the pleats, you get a true paper-bag effect and you can slide the skirt on and off without a zipper.

6. **Attach the facing.** With the right sides together and top edges and side seams aligned, stitch the facing to the top edge of the skirt. Press the seam allowance toward the facing and understitch (page 37). Hand-sew the facing to the zipper along the center-back opening.

7. **Fold and pin the pleats in place,** pressing the pleats from the top edge through the (marked) original waistline. Baste across the original waistline to secure the pleats in place.

8. **Assemble the sash.** With the right sides together and raw edges aligned, stitch the two sashes together, leaving an opening for turning. Clip the corners and turn the sash right side out. Press the sash, turning the seam allowance at the opening to the inside. Edgestitch around all the edges, closing the opening as you stitch.

9. **Hem the skirt.** Press under the bottom edge of the skirt ½" to the wrong side, then another 1". Topstitch close to the inner folded edge, or sew the hem as desired (pages 45–51).

10. **Add belt loops if desired.** This skirt has belt loops at the side seams to help hold the sash in place. For how to make and attach belt loops, see page 155.

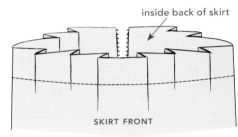

inside back of skirt

SKIRT FRONT

step 8

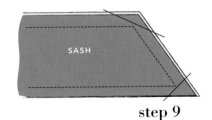

SASH

step 9

Tough Luxe Skirt

Design Variation: Asymmetrical Opening and Welt Pocket

The welt pocket is the most complicated pocket to sew; however, it's completely doable if you take your time. The "welts" refer to the two folds used to hold the pocket closed when it's not in use. The professional edge of these pockets will impress both fellow sewers and fashion lovers.

SATURDAY

Draft the Pattern

1. Trace your basic high-waisted skirt front and back patterns (page 199) onto drafting paper. Do not add any seam or hem allowances yet. Change the design to a one-dart silhouette (page 64).

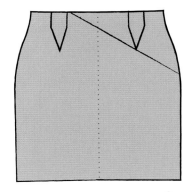

step 2a

2. **Draft the skirt front. a)** Trace the skirt front and then flip the pattern over so the center fronts are aligned and trace it again to draft a whole skirt front. Draw a design line as desired for the asymmetrical opening.

   b) Cut apart the skirt front along the opening. Cut the top pieces apart along the dart legs and label them as indicated. Add ½" seam allowance and 2" hem allowance.

3. **Place the pocket.** The pocket on this skirt is stitched about 5½" from the top edge. Draw a straight line equal in length to the desired pocket opening on the pattern at the desired location.

4. **Draft the bag for the welt pocket.** Draw the pattern twice as long as the desired pocket size + 1" (the pocket for this skirt is 5" wide × 4" long). Mark the center fold on the pattern. Then draw the pocket opening 1" below the center fold and ½" wide. The sides of the pocket opening should end ½" inside each side edge. Add ¼" seam allowance around the outside edges of the entire pocket.

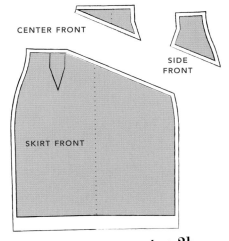

step 2b

PATTERN DRAFTING NOTE

A welt pocket can go anywhere on your skirt. Sometimes they are stitched parallel to the top edge of the skirt and sometimes they are at an angle. Look at the pockets on your clothing and in the stores for ideas. This welt pocket only requires one extra pattern piece. However, you do need to mark the pocket(s) placement on your pattern and you need to decide how wide and how long to make the pocket.

step 4

5. **Draft the skirt back.** Draft a vent (kick pleat) (pages 119–120) to complement the design elements on the front of the skirt, and to allow for walking.

6. **Draft the front and back facings.** Trace the top edge of all the pattern pieces (skirt front, center front, side front, back) and then draw a parallel line approximately 2" from the top edge to make the facing patterns. Trace the darts too, and then tape them closed to create the pattern pieces.

7. **Complete the pattern.** Add grainlines and registration marks to all of your pattern pieces (page 72). Add ½" seam allowance to all the pieces, except the pocket and three skirt front pieces.

Sew the Tough Luxe Skirt

1. **Cut out the fabric.** Use the newly drafted pattern pieces to cut the following:

   - *From fabric:* one skirt front, one center front, one side front, one skirt-front facing, one center-front facing, one side-front facing, one pocket bag, two skirt backs, and two back facings.

   - *From interfacing:* one of each facing.

2. **Apply interfacing.** Following the manufacturer's instructions, fuse the interfacing to the wrong side of all facings.

3. **Stitch the front and back darts** (page 35). Press them toward the center front and center back.

4. **Trace the pocket placement marking** from the pattern onto the skirt fabric (this line is equal to the desired pocket opening width) and mark each side of this line. Then measure out 1½" beyond each side marking and extend the pocket placement line. Trace the pocket markings on the pocket bag pattern onto the pocket bag fabric.

SUPPLIES

> **2 yards of 44/45" fabric**

> **½ yard of fusible interfacing**

> **11" zipper**

> **Zipper presser foot**

> **Matching thread**

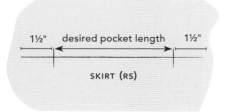

1½"   desired pocket length   1½"

SKIRT (RS)

step 4

5. **Attach the pocket. a)** Position the wrong side of the pocket bag over the pocket opening on the right side of the skirt with the pocket openings aligned. Baste the pocket bag in place through the center of the opening, as shown.

b) Machine-stitch around the pocket opening through both layers.

c) Carefully cut through both the pocket and the skirt over the basting stitches in the center of the pocket opening. Cut a V at each end as shown.

d) Turn the pocket to the wrong side of the skirt, taking care to fold the edges along the stitch lines. Press the opening.

6. **Create the welts a)** from the wrong side of the pocket by folding the pocket bag to create the welts to meet in the center of the opening. Press the pocket folds in place.

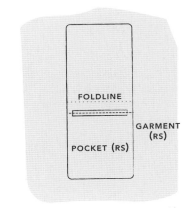

step 5a

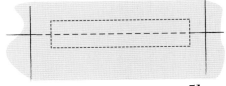

step 5b

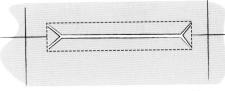

step 5c

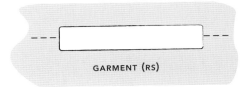

step 5d

step 6a

CONSTRUCTION NOTE
This method of making a welt pocket requires cutting into your skirt fabric to place the pocket. Make sure you double-check and triple-check the placement so you don't accidentally make a slash in the wrong place.

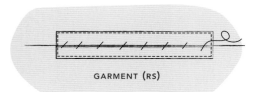

GARMENT (RS)

step 6b

b) Hand-baste the welts closed from the right side of the skirt. Then stitch in the ditch (see the tip on page 69) around the pocket opening through all the layers.

7. **Finish the pocket. a)** From the wrong side, fold the skirt away from the pocket at one side, exposing the ends of the welts. Machine-stitch (or hand-sew) the ends of the welts to the side edge of the pocket to secure the layers together. Repeat on the other side of the pocket.

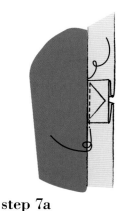

step 7a

b) Still from the wrong side, and to finish the pocket, fold the pocket bag in half (over the welt opening) so the right sides are together and the raw edges are aligned. Stitch around the edges of just the pocket with ¼" seam allowance. Remove the hand-basting stitches from step 6.

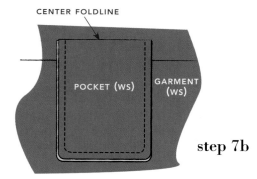

CENTER FOLDLINE

POCKET (WS)   GARMENT (WS)

step 7b

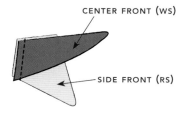

CENTER FRONT (WS)

SIDE FRONT (RS)

step 8

8. **Assemble the right top front edge of the skirt.** With the right sides together and inside edges aligned, stitch the center-front to the side-front. Press the seam allowances toward the side seam. Repeat with the facing pieces; however, press the facing seam allowances toward the center front.

9. **Insert an exposed zipper** in the seam of the asymmetrical opening, following the exposed zipper instructions on page 44.

10. **Center-back seam.** With the right sides together, stitch the center-back seam, adding a vent (kick pleat) (page 121).

11. **Sew the side seams.** With the right sides together and side seams aligned, stitch the skirt front to the back. Press the seam allowances open.

12. **Assemble the facing.** With the right sides together and raw edges aligned, stitch the back facings together at the center-back seam. Press the seam allowance open.

    With right sides together and the former dart sides aligned, stitch the center-front facing to the side-front facing.

    Then, with the right sides together and side seams aligned, stitch the two front facings to the assembled back facing. Press the seam allowances at the asymmetrical front openings to the wrong side.

    Press the seam allowance around the bottom edge of all facings ½" to the wrong side and topstitch to finish the edge.

13. **Attach the facing.** With the right sides together, raw edges aligned, and zipper open, pin the facing to the top edge of the skirt. Stitch the facing and skirt together. Press the seam allowance toward the facing and understitch (page 37). Hand-sew the facing to the zipper along the zipper opening and tack it to the skirt at the side seams.

14. **Hem the skirt.** Press under the bottom edge of the skirt ½" to the wrong side, then another 1½". Topstitch close to the inner folded edge, or hem as desired (pages 45–51).

INDEX

A

A-line, 45, 51, 161–62
appliqué, how to, 97
appliquéd skirt, 91–96
asymmetrical darts, 142–46
asymmetrical hemline (wrap skirt),
    102–6
asymmetrical opening, 228–33
awl, 20–21

B

back stitch (by hand), 28
basic straight seam, 31
basting stitch (by hand), 28
belt loops, 155
bias direction of fabric, 25
bias tape, how to make your own, 84
blind hem, machine-stitched, 48
Block Party Skirt, 138–41
bobbins, 14–15
body measurements, 54–55
box pleats, 181–84, 224–27
    inverted, 182–83, 216–19

bubble hemline, twisted, 189–92
button tab closure, 216–19
button-front closure, 123–28
drafting a button placket, 125
buttons and buttonholes, 38–39
    sew-through buttons, 38
    shank buttons, 39

C

catch stitch (by hand), 28
center fold, marking, 71
centered zipper, 40
clapper, 18–19
clean finish raw edges, 33–35
closures, 38–45
    buttons and buttonholes, 38–39
    hooks and eyes, 39
    snaps, 39
    zippers, 40–45
Coney Island Skirt, 205–10
contoured waistbands
    how to draft, 67
    on a wrap skirt, 80–83
contrast panels, 138–41

corners
    drafting right angles, 59
    how to sew, 35–36
crosswise grain, 25
curves
    how to sew, 36–37
    patternmaking tool, 20–21

D

darts
    asymmetrical, 142–46
    drafting a one-dart sloper, 64
    drafting darts on a sloper, 60–61
    how to sew, 35
    marking darts on a pattern, 72
decorated back pockets, 152–53
Dior, Christian, 117
Double-Time Wrap Skirt, 98–101
drafting a sloper, 56–62
    drawing the foundation, 56–57
    lengthen or shorten the skirt, 70
    lowering the waistline, 65
    marking, 56–62
    plotting one-dart sloper, 64
    plotting two darts, 60–61

taking measurements, 54–55
waistbands, 65–67
waistline and side seams, 58
waistline facing, 70
drafting paper, 21

E

edgestitching (by machine), 37
elasticized back waistband, 142–46
exposed zipper, 44–45, 220–23

F

fabric
  cutting, 25–26
  grain direction, 24–25
  identifying woven *vs.* knit, 24
  iron temperature settings, 26
  marking, 26
  preparing, 24
  right side and wrong side, 30

fabric marker, 14–15
faced
  hems, 49, 104
  pleats, 193–95
  waistline, 70, 185–88
flared skirts, 160–95
  adding extra flare, 165
  basic pattern, draft and sew, 162–64
  Girlie Show Skirt, 166–70
  Heavy Metal Skirt, 181–84
  Line-by-Line Skirt, 176–80
  Lone Star Skirt, 171–75
  New Twist Skirt, 189–92
  Piece Gathering Skirt, 185–88
  Violet Femme Skirt, 193–95
flared vertical panels, 176–80
flat-felled seam, 32
flounces, how to make, 112–15
French seam, 31
French Toast Skirt, 211–15
Frill Seeker Wrap Skirt, 111–15
front fly, 147–54
front hip pockets, 102–6, 123–25,
    147–54
full hemline, 166–70
full silhouettes, hemming, 45, 47

G

gathered waist, 166–70
gathering (by machine), 37
Girlie Show Skirt, 166–70
godets, 134–37
gored pockets, 211–15
grain direction, 24–25
Great Scot Skirt, 129–33
gridded pattern paper, 21

H-line, 117
hand stitches, 28
  hand-sewn hems, 49
Happy Hour Skirt, 216–19
Heavy Metal Skirt, 181–84
heavyweight fabrics, hemming, 46
hems, 45–51
  adding allowance to pattern, 71
  asymmetrical (wrap skirt), 102–6
  faced, 49, 104
  full silhouettes, 47
  hand-sewn, 49
  heavyweight fabrics, 46
  hem allowance for skirt type, 45
  machine-stitched blind hem, 48
  narrow hem, 48
  padded, 49
  reinforced with horsehair braid, 51
  scalloped (wrap skirt), 98–101
  topstitched, 46
  twisted bubble hemline, 189–92

High Definition Skirt, 134–37
high-waisted skirts, 196–233
  basic pattern, draft and sew, 198–200
  Coney Island Skirt, 205–10
  French Toast Skirt, 211–15
  Happy Hour Skirt, 216–19
  Hit the Sack Skirt, 224–27
  Jazz Age Skirt, 201–4
  Nip and Tuck Skirt, 220–23
  Tough Luxe Skirt, 228–33
hip curve, 21
hips, taking measurements, 54–55
Hit the Sack Skirt, 224–27
Hong Kong finish, 33
hooks and eyes, 39
horsehair braid, hems, 51, 204

Jazz Age Skirt, 201–4

kick pleat, 117
  drafting, 119–20
  sewing, 121
knife pleats, 129–33

in-seam pockets, 91, 93–94
interfacing
  how to apply fusible, 27
  how to attach sew-in, 27
  preparing before cutting, 24
inverted box pleats, 181–84, 216–19
invisible zipper, 41
iron and ironing board, 14–15
iron temperature settings, 26

lapped zipper, 42–43
lengthen a skirt pattern, how to, 70
lengthwise (or straight) grain, 25
Line-by-Line Skirt, 176–80
lining
  in a flared skirt, 176–80
  in a wrap skirt, 107–110
  making a twisted bubble hemline,
    189–92
  overlay and longer underlay, 171–75
  swing tack for securing, 29
Lone Star Skirt, 171–75

machine needles, 14–16
 types and sizes, 16
machine stitches, 37
machine-stitched blind hem, 48
marking
 fabric, 26
 patterns, 72
 tools for fabric, 26
 tools for patterns, 20–21
measurements how-to, 54–55
measuring tape, 20–21
military bellows pockets, 85, 87–90
muslin, how to make, 62–63

narrow hem, 48
needles, 14–16
 types and sizes, 16
New Twist Skirt, 189–92
New Wave Skirt, 142–46
Nip and Tuck Skirt, 220–23
notcher, 20–21
 how to mark a pattern, 71

overlay and longer underlay, 171–75

padded hem, 49
panels, ruched, 185–88
panels, vertical, 134–37
 flared, 176–80
paper-bag waistline, 224–27
patch pockets, 80, 82–83
patternmaking
 adding seam and hem allowance, 71
 tools, 20–21
pegged silhouette, 156–59
Piece Gathering Skirt, 185–88
pinking shears, 34
pins and pincushion, 14–15
piping
 adding to a flounce, 114–15
 presser foot attachment, 15
plackets, 125
pleats
 box and inverted box, 181–84
 faced, 193–95
 knife, 129–33
Pocket Change Skirt, 85–90
pockets

decorated back pockets, 152–53
front hip, 102–6, 123–25, 147–54
gored, 211–15
in-seam, 91, 93–94
military bellows, 85, 87–90
patch, 80, 82–83
welt, 228–233
point presser, 18–19
presser feet, 14–16
pressing
 fabrics and temperature settings, 26
 tools, 18–19

Quick Draw Skirt, 107–10

registration marks, how to make, 72
reinforced hem with horsehair braid, 51
reversible
 fabric, 134–37
 skirt, 98–101
ribbon
 waistband stay, 134–37, 180

right and wrong side of fabric, 30
ruched panels, 185–88
ruched waistband
  flared skirt, 171–75
  wrap skirt, 91–92, 95–96

S

sailor-style front opening, 205–10
sash, 224–27
scalloped hem, 98–101
scissors and shears, 14–15
seam allowance
  adding allowance to patterns, 71
  marking allowance on patterns, 72
  width, 30
seam edge, clean finish
  Hong Kong finish, 33
  pinking shears, 34
  serged or overlocked finish, 34
  topstitched edges, 34
  zigzag finish, 35
seam gauge, 14–15
seam ripper, 14–15
seams, how to sew
  basic straight seam, 31
  flat-felled seam, 32
  French seam, 31
selvage, 25–46
serged or overlocked finish, 34
sewing tools, 14–17
shorten a skirt pattern, how to, 70

slipstitch (by hand), 29
slit, 117
  drafting, 120
  sewing, 121
sloper, drafting a, 56–62
  drawing the foundation, 56–57
  lengthen or shorten the skirt, 70
  lowering the waistline, 65
  plotting one-dart sloper, 64
  plotting two darts, 60–61
  taking measurements, 54–55
  waistbands, 65–67
  waistline and side seams, 58
  waistline facing, 70
sloper, how to use, 73
snaps, 39
spiked tracing wheel, 20–21
Spot On Wrap Skirt, 80–84
Spring-Loaded Wrap Skirt, 74–115
stitch in the ditch, 33, 69
straight seam, 31
straight skirts, 116–59
  basic pattern, draft and sew,
    118–22
  Block Party Skirt, 138–41
  Great Scot Skirt, 129–33
  High Definition Skirt, 134–37
  New Wave Skirt, 142–46
  Super Fly Skirt, 147–54
  Twiggy Skirt, 123–28
  Velvet Crush Skirt, 156–59
Strong Suit Skirt, 102–6
Super Fly Skirt, 147–54
swing tack, 29

T

tailor's ham, 18–19
test skirt (muslin), 62–63
thread, 17
tools
  master tool list, 19
  patternmaking, 20–21
  pressing, 18–19
  sewing, 14–17
topstitched clean finish, 34
topstitched hem, 46
topstitching (by machine), 37
Tough Luxe Skirt, 228–33
tracing wheel, 20–21
transparent ruler, 21
trumpet silhouette, 201–4
tucks
  making, 107–10
  release, 220–23
Twiggy Skirt, 123–28
twisted bubble hemline, 189–92

U

underlay, 171–75
understitching (by machine), 37

vary form curve, 21
Velvet Crush Skirt, 156–59
vent, 117
  drafting, 119–20
  sewing, 121
vertical panels, flared, 176–80
Violet Femme Skirt, 193–95

waistbands
  assemble and attach, 68–69
  draft one-piece with separate facings,
    67
  draft two-piece contoured with sepa-
    rate facings, 67
  draft two-piece with separate facings,
    67
  elasticized back, 142–46
  ruched, on a wrap, 91–92, 95–96
waistline
  draft a facing, 70
  drafting a sloper, 58
  faced, 185–88
  gathered, 166–70
  lowering waistline on a sloper, 65
  paper-bag, 224–27

taking measurements, 54–55
waist stay made from ribbon, 134,
  137, 180
welt pockets, 228–233
whipstitch (by hand), 29
woven vs. knit, 24
wrap skirts, 74–115
  asymmetrical hemline, 102–6
  basic pattern, draft and sew, 76–79
  center-front opening, 85–90
  contoured waistbands, 67
  Double-Time Wrap Skirt, 98–101
  Frill Seeker Wrap Skirt, 111–15
  lining, 109–110
  Pocket Change Skirt, 85–90
  Quick Draw Skirt, 107–10
  reversible, 98–101
  ruched waistband, 91–92, 95–96
  Spot On Wrap Skirt, 80–84
  Spring-Loaded Wrap Skirt, 74–115
  Strong Suit Skirt, 102–6

yoke, straight skirt with a, 156–59

zigzag clean finish, 35
zippers, 40–45
  centered application, 40
  exposed application, 44–45
  invisible application, 41
  lapped application, 42–43

OTHER STOREY TITLES YOU WILL ENJOY

Fabric-by-Fabric One-Yard Wonders, by Rebecca Yaker and Patricia Hoskins.

101 more beautiful, stylish, and fun projects that use a diverse range of fabrics. 416 pages. Hardcover with concealed wire-o and patterns. ISBN 978-1-60342-586-5

Improv Sewing, by Nicole Blum and Debra Immergut.

A must-have guide that has 101 easy, beautiful freestyle sewing projects that can be created, embellished, and personalized in a single afternoon. 320 pages. Paper with flaps. ISBN 978-1-60342-740-1

One-Yard Wonders, by Rebecca Yaker and Patricia Hoskins.

101 hip, contemporary projects, from baby items and plush toys to pet beds and stylish bags, each made from just a single yard of fabric. 304 pages. Hardcover with concealed wire-o and patterns. ISBN 978-1-60342-449-3

Sew What! Bags, by Lexie Barnes.

Totes, messenger bags, drawstring sacks, and handbags — 18 pattern-free projects that can be customized into all shapes and sizes. 152 pages. Hardcover with concealed wire-o. ISBN 978-1-60342-092-1

Sew What! Skirts, by Francesca DenHartog & Carole Ann Camp.

A fast, straightforward method of sewing a variety of inspired skirts that fit your body perfectly, without relying on store-bought patterns. 128 pages. Hardcover with concealed wire-o. ISBN 978-1-58017-625-5

The Sewing Answer Book, by Barbara Weiland Talbert.

A friendly, reassuring resource that answers beginning and advanced sewing questions. 432 pages. Flexibind. ISBN 978-1-60342-543-8

These and other books from Storey Publishing are available wherever quality books are sold or by calling 1-800-441-5700. Visit us at **www.storey.com** or sign up for our newsletter at **www.storey.com/signup**.